CULTURE SMART!
BOLIVIA

Keith John Richards

·K·U·P·E·R·A·R·D·

First published in Great Britain 2009
by Kuperard, an imprint of Bravo Ltd
59 Hutton Grove, London N12 8DS
Tel: +44 (0) 20 8446 2440   Fax: +44 (0) 20 8446 2441
www.culturesmartguides.com
Inquiries: sales@kuperard.co.uk

Culture Smart! is a registered trademark of Bravo Ltd

Distributed in the United States and Canada
by Random House Distribution Services
1745 Broadway, New York, NY 10019
Tel: +1 (212) 572-2844   Fax: +1 (212) 572-4961
Inquiries: csorders@randomhouse.com

Copyright © 2009 Kuperard

Series Editor Geoffrey Chesler
Design Bobby Birchall

ISBN 978 1 85733 485 2

British Library Cataloguing in Publication Data
A CIP catalogue entry for this book is available from the
British Library

Printed in Malaysia

This book is available for special discounts for bulk purchases
for sales promotions or premiums. Special editions, including
personalized covers, excerpts of existing books, and corporate
imprints, can be created in large quantities for special needs.

For more information in the USA write to Special
Markets/Premium Sales, 1745 Broadway, MD 6–2, New York,
NY 10019, or e-mail specialmarkets@randomhouse.com.

In the United Kingdom contact Kuperard publishers at the
address at the top of this page.

Cover image: Bolivian textiles in market, La Paz. © iStockphoto.com

The photographs on pages 73, 75, 82, and 127 are reproduced by permission
of the author.

Images on the following pages reproduced under Creative Commons License
Attribution 2.5: 13 © Pattrön; 15 © Natalia Rivera; 18, 65 © Dr Eugen Lehle;
19, 47 © Christophe Meneboeuf; 24 © CNG; 41, 68, 80, 107, 125 © Elemaki/José Porras;
43 © Valter Campanato/ABr; 44 © Fabio Pozzebom/ ABr; 46 © Rodrigo Achá;
84 © Carlos Alberto Pacheco Patzi; 95, 113, 138 © marcalandavis; 98, 124 © Jerry
Daykin; 103 © Jenni Frog; 104 © Wilfredo R. Rodriguez H.; 114 © Franz Lozada;
116 © Alexson Scheppa Peisino; 117 © Micah MacAllen; 121 © Joel Alvarez;
126 © Jonathan Lewis; and 140 © Christopher Walker. Photo on page 137 © gaelj/fotolia

About the Author

KEITH JOHN RICHARDS was born in London in 1953. He has lived in Italy, Peru, Costa Rica, and the United States, as well as Bolivia. He received his Ph.D. in 1994 from King's College, University of London, for a thesis on the Bolivian novelist and historian Néstor Taboada Terán, which was published in 1999 as *Lo imaginario mestizo* (*The Mestizo Imaginary*). His critical bilingual anthology, *Narrative from Tropical Bolivia*, was published in 2004.

Keith Richards has taught Latin American film, literature, and popular culture at universities in Britain, the USA, and Bolivia. He has published widely on all these subjects and co-organized Latin American film symposia and festivals at the universities of Leeds (UK) and Richmond (Virginia). He has lived in La Paz, Bolivia, since 2005 and divides his time between teaching at the Universidad Mayor de San Andrés and writing; he is currently preparing a book on Latin American cinema.

contents

contents

Map of Bolivia

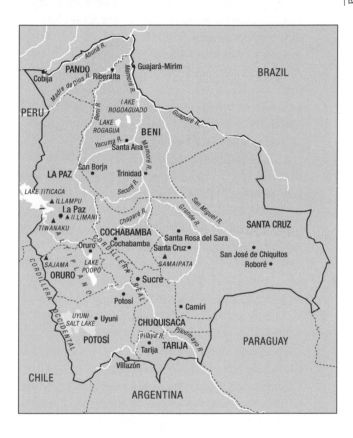

introduction

Bolivia is unique. For more than a century it has lacked a coastline, and few of its border regions differ in topography from its neighbors; the traveler passes into Chile and is still on the Altiplano, or enters Peru without losing sight of Lake Titicaca. Yet however capricious and arbitrary its borders may be, they help create a national psyche—if a divided one, with regional as well as national identities.

Part of Bolivia's uniqueness comes from the isolation that resulted from its becoming landlocked in the late nineteenth century, but its remoteness was evident even earlier. Even at its inception, it had only a tiny sea outlet in relation to its vast interior. It is through the process of emerging from isolation into dialogue with the rest of the world that some fascinating cultural and social changes are now occurring.

The stereotypical tourist image of Aymara women in bowler hats against a backdrop of snowy peaks is a constant source of frustration for the inhabitants of the lowlands and valleys, and is an indication that Bolivia's diversity is, even now, inadequately acknowledged. Bolivians are a mix of idiosyncrasies and inconsistencies: by turns open and inscrutable, generous with foreigners and tough with compatriots, self-abnegating and fiercely proud, stoical, and volatile. But warts are outweighed by virtues, and overall visitors find them good-humored, sociable, and welcoming. Despite their strong regionalism, they have more common interests than reasons to fight.

Bolivia is at a crossroads today. It has to find a way to become part of the modern world without surrendering its individuality, guaranteeing its people's growth and welfare while ensuring genuine benefits from its enormous natural wealth. It needs at last to cope with the regionalism that resists unification. It must learn to live with the vestiges of colonialism and banish the assumptions of racial inferiority that even today oppress the country's Indian majority.

Pessimistic observers see an innate capacity for self-destruction among Bolivians and point to repeated regional and ethnic conflict, but it should be remembered that this young nation contains oppressed minorities, some physically remote from the ruling elites, and others whose humanity is only now being acknowledged. These disparate elements have only recently begun to come into true contact. The demise of the Bolivian state, like the death of Mark Twain, has been grossly exaggerated—prophets of doom have underestimated the resilience of the people, their long experience of hardship, and their determination to overcome difficulties. What cannot be underestimated is their goodwill— "*!Bienvenidos a Bolivia!*" "Welcome to Bolivia."

Key Facts

Official Name	República de Bolivia	
Capital Cities	La Paz (seat of government); Sucre (official capital and seat of the judiciary)	
Main Cities	Santa Cruz (pop. 1,538,343); La Paz (pop. 839,905); El Alto (pop. 896,773); Cochabamba (pop. 603,342); Oruro (pop. 232,246)	
Area	424,164 sq. miles (1,098,581 sq. km)	
Terrain	Enormously varied landscape, including the Altiplano, or high plateau, in the west (at an average of 12,500 ft, or approx. 3,800 m); tropical rain forest in the east; subtropical valleys around Cochabamba and the Yungas forests north of La Paz	
Climate	Extremely varied: in west, dry and cold; hot and humid in the east	Altitude ranges from 21,463 ft (6,542 m) above sea level (Sajama) to 295 ft (90 m) (Río Paraguay).
Currency	Boliviano, or peso (100 centavos)	
Population	9,247,816 (July 2008)	
Life Expectancy	66.5 years	
Adult Literacy Rate	88.4%	
Ethnic Makeup	Quechua (30%), Mestizo (30%), Aymara (25%), European (15%)	
Official Languages	Spanish, Quechua, Aymara, Guaraní Some 30 other indigenous languages are considered "co-official."	

Religion	Catholic (88%), Protestant (6%), Baha'i (3%)	Indigenous religious beliefs are still strong in the countryside, though not organized.
Government	Bolivia is a multiparty democracy with a president (elected for a five-year term) as head of state and head of government.	There is no provision for a second round of voting: if no candidate gains 50% of the vote, a winner is decided by the National Congress.
Media	Various national TV channels, including P.A.T. and the state-run Canal 7. Several daily newspapers, including *La Razón, La Prensa* (La Paz), and *El Deber* (Santa Cruz)	No English-language newspapers or magazines
Electricity	220 volts, 60 Hz A/C. Older buildings may still have 110 volts, 50 Hz A/C.	European appliances need adaptors.
Telephone	Bolivia's country code is 59.	For intercity calls, dial the destination city code first. To phone abroad, dial 00 followed by the country code.
Internet Domain	.bo	
Television/Video	NTSC system	
Time Zone	Four hours behind Greenwich Mean Time (GMT -4)	From October to March GMT -3 (daylight saving time)

chapter one

LAND & PEOPLE

GEOGRAPHY

Lying at the heart of the South American continent, Bolivia borders the region's other landlocked country, Paraguay, to the southeast. It also shares frontiers with Peru and Chile to the west, Argentina to the south, and Brazil to the north and east.

Bolivia has a surface area almost twice that of Spain and slightly greater than the state of Texas: its population is about the same as Los Angeles County. Its population density is among the lowest in the world. Bolivia's surface area has diminished considerably since its foundation in 1825, but its extreme topographical diversity still makes it very difficult to administer as a coherent whole and to provide adequate communications. There are three main geographical zones: the Altiplano, the valleys, and the tropics.

The Altiplano (high plateau) was formed by the same seismic activity as the Andes; a huge section of seabed, the South American Plate, was lifted into its current position, an average of nearly 12,500 ft (approx. 3,800 m) above sea level, by the Nazca or Pacific Plate moving beneath it.

Marine fossils found there are often hawked to
tourists in the streets of La Paz. At the northern
end of the Altiplano lies Lake Titicaca, the highest
navigable body of water on earth, covering some
3,232 sq. miles (8,371 sq. km) and bisected by the
border with Peru. The Altiplano occupies the
western end of the country, spreading from
Titicaca to the borders with Chile to the west, and
with Argentina to the south. The area contains the
cities of La Paz, Oruro, and Potosí, as well as
mining areas that still produce tin, silver, and
other minerals. The altitude and extremes of
temperature make it a harsh environment.
Farmers cultivate potatoes and crops peculiar to
this habitat, such as *quinua*, *olluca*, and *cañahua*.
Llamas, once abundant here, are now gradually
giving way to sheep and cattle. The famous salt
lake at Uyuni is the world's largest.

The Andes, the planet's second-highest mountain range, date from the Cretaceous period (138–65 million years ago). The central Andean *cordillera*, or mountain chain, extends southwest across the western half of Bolivia. The highest peaks are Sajama (21,463 ft; 6,542 m) in the southwest, and Illimani (21,201 ft; 6,462 m), which overlooks the city of La Paz.

To the southeast of the Altiplano are the temperate valleys of Cochabamba, Chuquisaca, and Tarija. This hospitable area permits a broad spectrum of agricultural activity. The Cochabamba valley supplies the rest of the country with food.

The Chaco is an arid zone to the southeast shared with Argentina and Paraguay, to which countries Bolivia has lost considerable territory. This area contains most of the country's natural gas resources (exported to Brazil, gas is now the country's biggest earner) and still produces petroleum. The area's main river is the Pilcomayo, which flows some 1,550 miles (2,500 km) southeast from southern Bolivia into the Paraguay River just south of Asunción.

To the north and northwest are the tropics, the eastern lowlands (known as Oriente and Amazonía) that make up some three-fifths of Bolivia. The Mamoré is the most important river in this region, flowing north into the Madeira River in Brazil. Almost all its 1,180 miles (1,900 km) are navigable. The Guaporé forms part of the border with Brazil.

Much of the original forest has made way for soybean cultivation, particularly in the Santa Cruz area. Another activity in this area (with dubious ecological consequences) is cattle ranching.

The economy of the northern department of Pando long depended on rubber and was practically the private fiefdom of the "baron" Nicolás Suárez during the late nineteenth century (see the section on Melgarejo under "The Republican Era" below).

Departmental Capitals
Of Bolivia's nine departments, six (La Paz, Santa Cruz, Oruro, Cochabamba, Tarija, and Potosí) are named according to their capital cities. The exceptions are Beni (capital Trinidad), Pando (Cobija), and Chuquisaca (Sucre).

CLIMATE
Bolivia's climate is as varied as its geography, though there are really only two seasons: winter (April to October) and summer (November to March). The weather is becoming ever more unpredictable due to global warming, the El Niño effect, and other influences.

REGIONAL VARIATIONS

- Altiplano: the climate at this altitude would be very harsh if it were not for the region's latitude, keeping temperatures relatively benign. Summer is the rainy season. It occasionally snows on the Altiplano, if rarely in La Paz. Winter is cold but dry: despite the constant sunshine, air temperatures drop at night as the thin air does not retain warmth. Mean temperatures: summer 79°F (26°C), winter 59°F (15°C).

- Temperate valleys: agreeably warm days and cool nights, with rain in the summer months. Mean annual temperature: 62–80°F (17–27°C).

- Chaco: extremely hot and dry, except for the rainy season from December to April, when precipitation can reach over 23.6 inches (600 mm). Temperatures can rise as high as 115°F (46°C) in summer, and fall to less than -32°F (0°C) in the winter.

- Tropical lowlands: hot and wet. The Amazon basin (Pando and Beni) is hot and humid with high rainfall. The same applies largely to the southeastern lowlands (Santa Cruz department) although winters can be cooler, due mostly to the southern winds (*surazos*). Mean temperatures: summer 79°F (26°C); winter 59°F (15°C).

PEOPLE

Bolivia had 9,247,816 inhabitants in July 2008. Calculations of ethnic ratios differ, often for political reasons, and are largely dependent on self-perception. Most surveys indicate a ratio of roughly half indigenous, and half mestizo and white, though this is notoriously difficult to evaluate.

Part of Bolivia's historical problem in keeping control of its outlying regions can be attributed to the failure to populate these areas. Population distribution is still a problem today. Most people live in the west, which is the area least able to support human habitation, though there have been programs to populate areas such as the northern Pando and the Chapare near Cochabamba.

There have also been attempts to bolster the population by offering land to foreign immigrants: Mennonites arrived at various times in the twentieth century from places including Mexico, Paraguay, and Russia via Canada, to cultivate the Chaco and Beni, while Japanese and Croatian settlers were brought in to areas near Santa Cruz in the early twentieth century. There has been limited immigration from Germany, Spain, and Italy.

A BRIEF HISTORY

Bolivia has been shaped by myriad historical forces operating at different levels of intensity in the country's various regions. Here we shall attempt to pull together these numerous strands.

Pre-Columbian Bolivia

Opinion varies greatly as to the dates of the original settlement of the Americas. For some, this began with the Clovis culture of New Mexico, c. 13,500–12,500 BCE. Others hold that it slightly predates this, with a third school of thought placing the human presence at about 30,000 BCE. According to this estimate, the Bolivian Andes would have been populated as long as 20,000 years ago. Established civilizations have existed in Bolivia for perhaps three millennia, but their importance is not yet appreciated.

Bolivian Andean archaeology is generally divided into three main Horizons. The Early (Chavín) Horizon (1400–400 BCE) saw the emergence of trade and interchange between the region's cultures and those of other parts of South America, leading to the formation and consolidation of settled societies. The most important development was the invasion by people from the Chavín region of central Peru—

an influence seen during the Early Middle Horizon (400 BCE–500 CE). The Middle Horizon (500–900 CE) is also named the Tiwanaku, because that culture's sophistication, power, and influence reached its zenith during this period, alongside that of the Huari culture in Peru. The degree of association between these two cultures has yet to be determined, as have the reasons for Tiwanaku's decline. The years 900–1476 are the Late Middle Horizon. During the Late Horizon (1476–1534), the Incas incorporated the area into their realm of political control and cultural influence; this process was truncated by the Spanish invasion.

Archaeological work in Bolivia is still far from complete, reflecting the neglect of pre-Columbian indigenous cultures until recently. One of those who encouraged interest in this heritage was Vienna-born Arthur Posnansky (1873–1946), whose unbounded praise of the indigenous Aymara people as an Andean "master race" was both eccentric and politically questionable. Posnansky's nationalist feeling for Bolivia was such that he fought against Brazil in the Acre War (1899–1902). He saw the ruins of Tiwanaku, near Lake Titicaca, as a potential national symbol along the lines of Machu Picchu in Peru or Mexico's Aztec ruins.

Until the 1950s, most archaeological activity had been undertaken by foreigners such as Posnansky, Max Ühle, and Dick Ibarra Grasso. The great

exception is Carlos Ponce Sanginés, generally
considered the father of Bolivian archaeology.
His work mainly focuses on Tiwanaku, the most
intriguing of Bolivian pre-Columbian sites. Ponce
Sanginés identified five phases in Tiwanaku,
culminating in a classic period when it controlled an
area stretching from today's Cochabamba to southern
Peru. It is thought to date from around 1500 BCE and
to have been in decline by 1200 CE. Tiwanaku
dominated and at times physically relocated
populations such as the Urus and the Chipayas.

The Finnish archaeologist Martti Pärssinen has
undertaken work to show that Bolivia's lowland
cultures were not only part of an intricate network
that linked them with the Andes but that they were
of great sophistication in their own right.

Samaipata, one of the chief archaeological sites
in the east of the country, lies between Santa Cruz
and Cochabamba. It features a single huge carved
rock that is generally believed to have been a
ceremonial site.

The Spanish Conquest
The territory now known as Bolivia was conquered
and colonized from two almost diametrically
opposite directions: Lake Titicaca in the west, and the
Plate River (Río de la Plata) in the southeast. In both
cases, the Spaniards were spurred on by the prospect
of reaching the fabled land of El Dorado—otherwise
known, in this region, as Gran Paitití (meaning and
origin unclear).

In 1531 the Spaniards reached the Peruvian coast. Within a couple of years of their arrival in the Inca capital, Cuzco, they had destroyed the infrastructure of a civilization that, though not lasting particularly long, was remarkable for its organization and coherence. The southern part of the Inca territory Tawantinsuyo ("union of four quarters" in Quechua, the Inca lingua franca) was the Kollasuyo, the origin of the modern nickname "*colla*" used for Andeans. The Spaniards could simply follow the Incas' path southward, forming alliances with local peoples who wished to rid themselves of their imperial masters, unaware that they were making way for something far worse.

The Spanish navigator Juan Díaz de Solís had reached the mouth of the Plate River on the Atlantic in 1516, but was ambushed and killed when attempting to find a passage to the Pacific by sailing up it. The Guaraní-speaking Chiriguano cultures to the east were largely comprised of Amerindians seeking what their mythology had determined as a "Land without Evil"—a coincidence with the El Dorado sought by the Spaniards, leading to a sometimes curious conjunction of forces. "Chiriguano" is said to be a pejorative Quechua term used by the populations resettled by the Incas to refer to the locals.

The area to the northwest of Santa Cruz was largely settled by Jesuit missions, which served as frontier outposts for the Spanish presence. This, however, does not mean the absence of conflict: the city of Santa Cruz de la Sierra, founded in 1561 by Ñuflo de Chávez, who had penetrated inland from Buenos Aires, was moved at least twice due to environmental factors and hostility from local peoples, finally settling in its current site in 1592.

The Colonial Era
The Viceroyalty of Peru, created in 1542, controlled the first incarnation of today's Bolivia, Upper Peru. Peru's predominance in South America was undermined by the creation of two new Viceroyalties, first Nueva (New) Granada in 1717, then Plate River (Río de la Plata) in 1776. These new entities shifted political and economic influence from Lima to Caracas and Buenos Aires.

The Royal Audience of Charcas, based in the city of La Plata (now Sucre), was a judicial and administrative body created by Philip II of Spain in 1559 to rule Upper Peru. The city's university, San Francisco Xavier, paradoxically produced some of the region's foremost revolutionaries.

In 1570, the Spaniards put a definitive end to Inca rule with the execution of Tupac Amaru I. Tupac Amaru had been a symbolic figure reduced to a clandestine existence—his chief gesture of resistance, apparently, his refusal to convert to Christianity.

The Potosí *Mita*

The discovery in 1543 of a huge vein of silver at Potosí, some 341 miles (550 km) south of La Paz, was to have major consequences for the history of the region. In 1545 a city was founded in this hostile area, 13,123 ft (approx. 4,000 m) above sea level, which had to be supplied and serviced from the surrounding valleys. At first the mined silver was smelted by Indian craftsmen, an activity later taken over by the Crown. In the 1570s Viceroy Toledo brought in

measures to rationalize silver production in Potosí, dividing the city into white and Indian sectors, and setting up the infamous *mita* (labor tribute).

These measures acknowledged that it was imperative to use Indian labor to extract the metal. Because the enslavement of Native American peoples was technically banned by the

Crown (largely as a result of campaigns by humanitarian churchman Bartolomé de las Casas), an alternative had to be found. Black slaves, it was discovered, died all too easily in the cold, rarified air of Potosí: in any case, they were extremely expensive to bring in and were used largely as servants—a status symbol in rich people's homes. This dilemma led the Spanish to revive the ancient Inca practice of exacting *mita* from the populace—but with a difference. Whereas under Inca rule the people saw some of the benefits of the *mita*, the Spaniards used it for their own enrichment, and to great effect.

As news spread of the extraordinary wealth of Potosí, people flocked to the city from all over the globe to seek their fortune. Potosí was also where peoples from different regions of the Iberian peninsula met for the first time—these were not always peaceful encounters, as can be seen from the so-called Vicuña Wars of the 1620s, which pitted Spanish newcomers against Creoles (*criollos*: people of Spanish descent, born in the Americas). It is estimated that, by the seventeenth century, Potosí was the most populous city in the Western hemisphere.

The Rebellion of Tupac Katari and the Katarismo Movement

There was an Indian uprising in the Cuzco area of Peru (1780–82) led by Gabriel Condorcanqui, who

styled himself Tupac Amaru II. Another revolt, in
the department of Potosí, broke out when the rural
mayor Tomás Catari protested at a rise in the
already onerous tribute demanded by the Spanish.
Yet another rebellion (1780–81) was led by Julián
Apaza, whose *nom de guerre* Tupac Katari combined
elements of both his predecessors' names.

Apaza, supported by his wife Bartolina Sisa and
his sister Gregoria, aimed to set up Indian self-
government, advancing a notion of cultural purity
that included the obligatory use of Aymara. His
forces surrounded La Paz on March 13, 1781, and
blockaded the huge valley for some three months,
almost starving out the inhabitants. The siege
enhanced the image of Indian women as organizers
and fighters: Bartolina Sisa, Gregoria Apaza, and
others are still fêted today. When reinforcements
arrived from Chuquisaca, the Spaniards were able
to capture the couple and cruelly execute them.
Tupac Katari, like Tupac Amaru II in Peru, was
quartered using horses. His reported last words, "I
will come back, as millions," are often quoted today.

These great rebellions took two years to put
down, severely undermining the Spaniards'
confidence in their ability to retain control in
the Americas.

The 180th anniversary of Tupac Katari's death
was commemorated in 1961 by the foundation of
a radical study group set up to investigate the
experience of the Indians since the conquest, and
how it had affected them. This association of

students grew into the intellectual current known as "Katarismo," in which a separatist, anti-white tendency was overcome by a more realistic faction advocating the struggle of exploited versus exploiters.

Katarismo has undergone many changes associated with educational politics as well as, briefly, armed struggle. It has been of huge importance and contributed to many parties and social movements, including today's governing MAS (Movement Toward Socialism).

Independence
The sense of insecurity created in 1781 was to prove justified: La Paz was again the site of a mutiny when, on July 16, 1809, rebels called for an end to Spanish rule. This revolt was swiftly put down and its leaders executed in January 1810, but it inspired other similar movements in Buenos Aires and Quito. This time the insurrection was united: Indians, mestizos, and Creoles joined forces.

A number of districts throughout Upper Peru, from Potosí to Santa Cruz, declared themselves independent "small republics" (*republiquetas*) and had some limited success in resisting the Spanish. The most important center of guerrilla warfare was the *republiqueta* of Ayopaya, on the Altiplano. This was also seen as a threat by the Creole landowning oligarchy; the guerrilla commander, José Miguel García Lanza, was killed before he had the opportunity to take power. Theories vary as to what might have developed had the Ayopaya uprising not been snuffed out. After Argentine liberator General San Martín's success in Peru, culminating in his victory over the remaining royalist forces at Ayacucho and Junín in 1824, Bolivia's independence was declared in 1825.

The Republican Era

As has often been pointed out, the change from Spanish colony to independent state benefited only a small minority of Creole families. For the great majority of ordinary Bolivians, things were to remain the same or get even worse.

The 1809 events in La Paz, the first Latin American city to demand independence from Spain, were crucial in the region's independence movement. The Republic of Bolivia was founded on August 6, 1825, its territory based on that of Charcas. There were originally five administrative areas (later denominated departments): Cochabamba, Santa Cruz de la Sierra, La Paz, Potosí, and Chuquisaca. Oruro, Tarija, Beni, and Litoral (the coastal department lost to Chile) were added later. The first president was Antonio José de Sucre (1795–1830), who was elected in 1826 but resigned in 1828.

The republican era in Bolivia was marked by further wars, the War of the Pacific (1879–93) and the Acre War (1899–1902). It also saw the exploration of national territory for scientific investigation, missionary activity, prospecting, and the inevitable military adventurism. Oil, rubber, and other natural resources were sought by foreigners with adequate economic backing.

During the nineteenth and early twentieth centuries, La Paz and Sucre were extremely remote from Santa Cruz and the Oriente: those few people who made their fortunes in rubber or ranching found it easier and quicker to travel to Europe than to visit their own national capital.

This was also a time during which the power of rural Indian clan-based communities, or *ayllus*, was reduced, due to their emphasis on reciprocity and community ownership. Left-leaning thinkers saw them as the basis for a possible Andean socialism, whereas the oligarchy used their supposedly "communist" characteristics as a convenient pretext to justify land expropriations.

Mariano Melgarejo (1818–71), Bolivia's most controversial president before Evo Morales, held office from 1864 to 1871, and is often blamed for the loss of Acre province to Brazil. Tales of Melgarejo's brutality and ignorance are rife but difficult to substantiate; what is beyond doubt is that he had powerful enemies who objected to his race and class. The reactionary novelist Alcides Arguedas dismissed Melgarejo as a *cholo* (unlike the feminine form *chola*, which refers to a socially respected figure, this is a racist term for a semi-acculturated Indian or mestizo), and a disgrace to the office of president. Melgarejo was assassinated in Lima in 1871 after having left power.

Some of the tales about Melgarejo are clearly apocryphal. For example, it is said that he humiliated the British ambassador and banished him from the country. When news of this reached Buckingham Palace, an enraged Queen Victoria had Bolivia removed from the map of South America and condemned to oblivion. A picturesque anecdote, but historians have pointed out that Britain did not even have diplomatic representation in Bolivia at the time. Although the story was circulated by enemies of Melgarejo keen to discredit him, it nevertheless contains a true reflection of Bolivia's feeling of vulnerability to the whims of imperial powers. In the case of the British Empire, such suspicions were justified.

The rubber baron Nicolás Suárez (1851–40) became immensely rich and his fortunes were inextricably linked to those of the department of Pando. Rocketing rubber prices toward the end of the nineteenth century created tensions between Bolivia, Peru, and Brazil, which erupted in the Acre War (1899–1902). The Acre region, rich in rubber and gold deposits, was ceded to the

Brazilians once again. The inaccessibility of its own territory was Bolivia's undoing.

The "Dismemberment"

Bolivia's history has been stained by a long succession of military disasters and other instances of gross mismanagement, exacerbated by the voracity of South American neighbors aided by world superpowers. Whereas some of these losses have resulted from shady diplomacy and Bolivia has received concessions or recompense, others have been military debacles that have seen the country's territory almost halved to its current 424,164 sq. miles (1,098,581 sq. km).

In the catastrophic War of the Pacific (1879–83) Bolivia lost its entire coastal Litoral province (46,332 sq. miles; approx. 120,000 sq. km) to Chile.

The protracted dispute and conflict (1899–1903) over Acre province, in the northern lowlands, ended

in 1903, when Bolivia ceded almost 60,000 sq. miles (approx. 155,399 sq. km) of territory rich in rubber to Brazil. Bolivia also surrendered 19,300 sq. miles (approx. 50,000 sq. km) of the Matto Grosso on its eastern borders in 1928 to Brazil.

The Chaco War with Paraguay (1932–35) resulted in the loss of the southeastern area of the Chaco Boreal (90,300 sq. miles; approx. 234,000 sq. km).

In 1899 Bolivia ceded the Puna de Atacama to Argentina, which in return renounced its claim to the southern Bolivian province of Tarija. Chaco Central passed into Argentine hands in 1920.

The Twentieth Century

By the early twentieth century Sucre was a backwater despite being the national capital—a status claimed by the more thrusting La Paz. A civil war between the two cities in 1898 saw Indians used by local leaders as cannon fodder. The indigenous leader Pablo Zárate Willka (nicknamed "*el Temible*," the Fearsome) obtained promises of restitution of Indian lands in return for Quechua and Aymara support for the La Paz cause. Willka's forces helped La Paz to victory, but their erstwhile allies reneged on the deal. The Indians tried to grab what they had been promised, but Willka and other leaders were imprisoned and eventually murdered.

The Federalists won this civil war, but instead of the planned creation of a federal republic with La Paz as its capital, they reached a compromise: Sucre remained the official capital and the seat of judicial power, and La Paz became the seat of government and parliament. This situation is still disputed today for political ends, Sucre demanding full status as capital as a way to undermine the Morales government.

The pointless slaughter of the Chaco War with Paraguay (1932–35) saw thousands of peasants perish in the hostile Chaco Boreal. President Daniel Salamanca justified the conflict as an opportunity to counterbalance Bolivia's history of international disasters with a victorious war. Salamanca omitted to mention pressure from US Standard Oil, in opposition to Paraguay-based UK company Royal Dutch Shell, both of which were vying to exploit rights in the territory.

The Chaco trauma led to a shakeup of Bolivia's social structure that has yet to be fully resolved. *Campesino* (peasant farmer) unionism sprang up in Cliza, near Cochabamba, in response to abuses such as summary evictions and usurpations of lands occupied by families whose men were away fighting.

During the war Salamanca and his successor, José Luis Tejada Sorzano, were both removed in coups masterminded by Colonel Germán Busch. Colonel David Toro was installed as head of a civilian-military junta whose political orientation was described as "military socialism." Newly organized

Indian unions won rights to rent convent land and establish rural schools. But landowners refused to accept such demands and counterattacked. Busch ousted Toro in 1937, with the declared aim of furthering military socialism, and replaced him with General Carlos Quintanilla, who was far more amenable to the oligarchy's interests. Busch died suddenly in 1939—apparently it was suicide.

The right reasserted itself under General Enrique Peñaranda (1940–43), who was in turn removed by another reformist military regime under Major Gualberto Villarroel, under whom the first indigenous congress was convened to contain the burgeoning *campesino* movement. Analysts have yet to agree on Villarroel's true political sympathies; his measures included recognizing trade unions and granting workers' rights to schools and pensions. But workers continued to defy the oligarchs, withholding all feudal-style free service while the strikes continued. Villarroel's government was eventually squeezed between the demands of left and right: he was overthrown and murdered in the Plaza Murillo in July 1946.

A succession of pro-oligarchy presidents continued to repress, or try to ignore, the increasingly powerful claims of workers and *campesinos*. The Catavi massacre of 1942, the agricultural strikes of 1941–43, and the ever-larger demonstrations and uprisings were not enough to convince landowners and industrialists that change was imminent and inevitable.

The National Revolution

Campesino uprisings ensued in 1947 as a response
to the landowners' intransigence, and were met
with further repression. The 1951 elections were
won by the MNR (Revolutionary Nationalist
Movement) but the outgoing president Mamerto
Urriolagoitia (the last civilian of the old oligarchy
to hold the position) expressed the
establishment's resentment of the MNR by
handing power to the armed forces under Hugo
Ballivián and annulling the election.

In April 1952 the events subsequently known as
the National Revolution occurred. The MNR had
formed a pact with a government figure, General
Antonio Seleme, to take power. The army's
attempt to stifle this was opposed by popular
militias and hunger strikes. The Revolution
prevailed, with relatively little bloodshed, as many
conscripts were simply persuaded not to fight.
The army was dissolved (it was refounded in July
1953) and the trade union COB (Bolivian
Workers' Central) was established.

Universal suffrage was at last introduced, with
80 percent of the population suddenly empowered

and no longer treated as beasts
of burden. However, many
observers felt that some of the
measures adopted by the MNR
were inadequate (though they
did try to address the country's
most pressing problems): they were either applied

without conviction, bowed too much to US pressure, or else were used by MNR members as opportunities for self-enrichment.

Agrarian reform, for example, was complicated by the fact that some MNR members belonged to the very landowning class that was to be dispossessed. Compensation for expropriated land was thought excessive by *campesinos*, who were also unhappy with the small plots they were offered. Larger portions than this were granted per head of cattle to ranchers in the Oriente; in fact large landholdings granted to friends of a series of political leaders are still a source of unrest today as the MAS government seeks to implement fairer land distribution. Radical *campesino* leaders were either jailed or co-opted by means of bribes, while rural unions were manipulated by MNR members. The Aymara and Quechua cultural heritage was undervalued and ancestral agricultural methods were not respected. Indians in the Oriente fared worse, being officially classed as minors.

In July 1956 Hernán Siles was elected to succeed Paz Estenssoro as president, but Siles encountered problems with MNR factionalism, worker opposition, inflation, and disarming the militias.

In 1960 Paz Estenssoro was again elected, and he applied measures proposed by a White House keen to avoid another Cuba. In 1964 Paz Estenssoro won yet again, but factionalism within the MNR and uncertainty over the revolution's aims culminated in a military coup that year led by Vice President

René Barrientos, whose "military–*campesino* pact" pragmatically consolidated his own power and defused potentially dangerous rural opposition. The pact did not mean unconditional respect for *campesino* and workers' rights, however, as was clear from the army's brutal repression of a mine rebellion in the 1967 "San Juan" massacre.

Suppression of the Left and the Rise of García Meza

The sudden death of Barrientos in 1969 permitted an interval of socialist rule under General Juan José Torres (1970–71), who attempted to introduce radical changes for which the country was unprepared. Distrusted by both left and right, he was ousted in August 1971 by another coup, led by Hugo Banzer. Supported by the US and the Brazilian dictatorship of the time, this was a far more typical military regime. Between 1971 and 1978 all leftist political parties and institutions, including the COB, were suspended. During this era of juntas across Latin America, Banzer did not lack political and logistical support.

However, even this regime had its problems. In 1974 financial difficulties led Banzer to take tough economic measures that provoked demonstrations. Banzer declared a state of siege that only heightened the unrest. His downfall was precipitated by a hunger strike, led by an extraordinarily courageous and lucid women's leader from the mines, Domitila Chungara (see Further Reading).

"CHE"

The death of Argentine revolutionary Ernesto "Che" Guevara in December 1967 is a key moment in Bolivian history. Guevara's choice of Bolivia as the focus for his revolutionary movement remains puzzling. He apparently thought the movement would spread outward across Bolivia's numerous borders. However, he completely miscalculated the prevailing mentality in sparsely populated eastern Bolivia, evidently expecting to find the same degree of political awareness as in the militant mining areas of the west. Bolivia had had a revolution only fourteen years earlier, but remote areas were still extremely conservative and it was easy for the authorities to mobilize opposition to the guerrillas, demonized as foreign communists out to kill Bolivians and steal their cattle. Che's group was eventually surrounded in the area of Vallegrande, and he was summarily shot in the village of La Higuera.

Today the area is a tourist destination:

Che is both a merchandising emblem and a genuine example of revolutionary passion and sacrifice. In conservative Santa Cruz he is invisible: in Andean cities his face is painted on myriad city walls, buses, and other public spaces.

The Carter administration pressured Banzer to restore democracy, but his reluctance to comply led to a far worse dictatorship. Luis García Meza is a name that still sends shivers up Bolivian spines. His "narco-dictatorship," with its barely concealed links to drug trafficking, was mercifully short (1980–81) but extremely brutal.

García Meza is one of few former dictators to have been caught and tried: in 1986 he was sentenced to thirty years in the high-security Chonchocoro prison. Among his illustrious victims were two opponents of authoritarianism: Marcelo Quiroga Santa Cruz, founder of the Bolivian Socialist Party and one of Bolivia's finest writers, who was preparing a legal case against Banzer for human rights abuses, was murdered during the coup on July 17, 1980; and Father Luis Espinal, an influential Catalan Jesuit priest, teacher, and intellectual, was captured, tortured, and finally killed on March 22, 1980.

The Slow Return to Democracy
The return to formal democracy came in 1982, when Hernán Siles returned as president with the leftist Popular Democratic Union, but this government was hampered by severe economic problems and hostile opposition on both left and right. Having achieved the arrest and expulsion of Nazi war criminal Klaus Barbie, President Siles was kidnapped by police and army officers in June 1984 in an attempted coup. Inflation continued to

spiral, reaching a staggering 8,265,000 percent in 1985. That same year Siles was replaced once more by Paz Estenssoro, whose attempt to tackle hyperinflation was hamstrung by the collapse in tin prices in 1985. More than 23,000 miners lost their jobs: this proved the end of an era as regards miners' political power.

Despite most of the votes going to Gonzalo Sánchez de Lozada's MNR in the 1989 election, power was shared between the third-placed Jaime Paz Zamora's MIR (Revolutionary Left Movement) and the runner-up, former dictator Banzer's ADN (Democratic Nationalist Action). Banzer had persecuted and murdered members of the MIR, but now the former sworn enemies were allies. This government (1989–93) achieved a measure of economic control, and relaxed certain political tensions. For example, it recognized native rights to ancestral lands after the 1990 Indigenous March for Land and Dignity.

Sánchez de Lozada's first government (1993–97) included the Aymara activist Víctor Hugo Cárdenas as the country's first indigenous vice president. "Goni" (to use the once-popular nickname) could list numerous achievements, including provision for bilingual education, the "Popular Participation" law enabling a certain amount of local autonomy and decentralization, as well as

constitutional and legal reforms. Goni's most controversial step was the capitalization (a form of privatization) of five major state companies. But there was considerable social unrest and confrontation during this government, leading to a state of siege lasting for six months.

While there has been little prospect of a return to military rule, Banzer's return to power in 1997 was a reminder of both the nostalgia for authoritarianism, on the part of many voters, and the nature of the Bolivian electoral procedure. Banzer's "election" was achieved with a minority vote but the support of Congress, since there is no provision for a second round of voting.

The second Banzer presidency had to cope with several problems: corruption scandals, the fallout from the detention of former Chilean dictator Pinochet in London in 1998, and an economic crisis at home. In the so-called "Water War" (2000) the population of Cochabamba successfully contested water privatization. Banzer died of cancer in 2002 at the age of seventy-five, after offering an inadequate and belated apology to those who "believed they were his victims." His vice president, Jorge "Tuto" Quiroga, who ruled from 2001 to 2002, later founded the PODEMOS party, routed in the 2005 election by Morales's MAS.

The "Gas War"
In February 2003 Goni's move to increase taxes was greeted with fury, and led to further unrest

throughout the country. The most politically far-
reaching example of popular resistance to fiscal
policy was the "Gas War" of October 2003 in
which the inhabitants of El Alto rejected Goni's
proposal to sell Bolivia's gas supplies to the United
States and Chile. The fury and resentment caused
by this plan can be explained as follows: it would
have benefited two of the countries seen as most to
blame for Bolivia's economic and political woes,
and continued a policy of selling off raw materials
at rock-bottom prices with little or no benefit to
the country's poorest and neediest people. The Gas
War resulted in the deaths of some sixty-seven
people at the hands of the military. Sánchez de
Lozada was forced to resign and fled the country.
Still wanted for human rights abuses (he ordered
the repression), he now lives in Florida.

Rachel Boynton's film *Our Brand is Crisis* traces
the undeniably effective role played by US public
relations company GCS in Goni's 2002 electoral

campaign. This contrasts with the disastrous consequences of Goni's second presidency. Interviews in Boynton's film show crestfallen GCS people unable to explain their man's abject failure and admitting the perils of marketing, however expertly, a valueless product in an environment of which they know nothing.

Goni's vice president, Carlos Mesa, took over. An urbane, well-spoken journalist and author, he was unable to convince or pacify the country in any way. These years of perceived misrule exacerbated what was already a profound distrust of the country's "political class," creating the conditions for the electoral success of Evo Morales and the MAS.

Evo Morales and the Movement Toward Socialism (MAS)

Evo Morales Ayma, the son of Aymara *campesinos*, was born in 1959 in Orinoca, on the Altiplano near Oruro. He had an impoverished rural childhood, with minimal schooling. After taking various jobs and doing basic studies in Oruro, Morales joined the large-scale migration to the Chapare that had begun in earnest in the 1970s, becoming a cultivator of coca and a union leader. As leader of the MAS, his election to the presidency of Bolivia in December 2005, with 54 percent of the vote, was the largest majority since another Indian candidate, the poet and essayist Franz Tamayo, was fraudulently denied office in 1934 after winning 59.2 percent of the vote.

Despite this undeniable weight of support, bolstered by a referendum held in August 2008, Bolivian society is split down the middle over Morales's mandate. Part of the opposition is because of his ethnic and social origins, though few opponents would admit to racism, often prefacing their remarks with the words, "Evo isn't even a true Indian."

From the outset there have been campaigns, orchestrated by landowners intent upon retaining their massive properties, to unsettle and discredit the government. The Morales regime has also been criticized by the left, which accuses it of collaborating with the bourgeoisie and transnationals. The vehemence of the opposition to Morales among landowners in the lowland provinces is clear from the "Porvenir massacre" of September 2008, in the northern department of Pando, where peasants demonstrating their support for MAS were murdered by paramilitaries under the then prefect, Leopoldo Fernández.

The current vice president, Álvaro García Linera, is another remarkable figure and a contrast to Morales. A white, middle-class intellectual with a degree in mathematics from Mexico City, García Linera has always been associated with Bolivia's radical indigenous movements. In 1992 he was jailed for four years for his part in blowing up an

electricity pylon as a member of the Tupak Katari Guerrilla Army (Ejército Guerrillero Tupak Katari, or EGTK). During his prison term he studied sociology, graduating after his release in 1997. After gaining a reputation as one of Bolivia's most lucid social and political commentators, he joined the MAS 2005 electoral campaign.

Among many bones of contention in the conflict between the government and the lowland departments is the IDH (Direct Hydrocarbons Tax), which is partly used to fund the old-age pension.

BOLIVIA TODAY

Bolivia has long been derided for its legendary political instability, and not without reason: eight of its presidents have been assassinated (three of them while no longer in office) and five have resigned. Today, however, the country has enjoyed more than a quarter century of elected government, with none of the military coups that plagued the 1960s and '70s.

Bolivia has gone through great changes in the past couple of decades, and is still a nation in transformation. Vestiges of its feudal past and subservience to foreign interests are still visible, however. The same can be said of a colonial mentality that surfaced in Sucre in May 2008, when *campesinos* demonstrating in favor of the Morales government were rounded up, humiliated, and whipped by an anti-MAS group: this genuinely shocked many people and remains controversial.

Some *haciendas* (large estates), particularly in the Chaco region, still effectively operate a feudal system, with workers tied to the land. The vast tracts of tropical lowland that are still owned by a handful of families favored during MNR and military rule present a particularly intractable problem that is still causing strife.

Industrialization is in its infancy, but is essential if the country is to escape its dependency on the sale of raw materials. While some progress has been made in health and education, there is still much to do before Bolivia can be regarded as a modern egalitarian state.

Government
Bolivia has a bicameral Congress, with 130 members in the House of Representatives and 27 in the Senate. The president, elected for five years by universal suffrage, may be reelected for only one nonconsecutive term. Such is Evo Morales's current popularity (his approval rating in the August 10, 2008, referendum was 70 percent) that this is now under review.

Suffrage was originally limited to men, and even then with certain restrictions, depending on the

local authorities. Voters had to be literate, responsible individuals who avoided drunkenness, vagrancy, and indecent behavior. In 1938 the vote was extended to women, under similar conditions. The literacy stipulation effectively excluded most indigenous people, though they might accede to citizenship, and hence suffrage, through education. Partly for this reason rural schools were, at first, energetically suppressed.

The MAS government won approval for its new constitution in a referendum on January 25, 2009. Implementation of the values enshrined in the document will entail a protracted legislative process and negotiation with departmental prefects. The approved constitution sets a limit for landholdings at 5,000 hectares (19.5 square miles) and enshrines the right of all citizens to education, health, and employment. Despite the lowland departments' rejection of the constitution, the absence of violence during the referendum was welcomed as possibly a new beginning for a country that has finally accepted the need for cooperation among its diverse social, regional, and ethnic constituents.

The Economy

Bolivia is finally beginning to enter a phase of industrialization, which offers the hope that it may be able to enjoy the fruits of its own natural resources. Opponents of Morales derided his 2006 nationalization of gas and oil reserves, arguing that the country lacked the necessary processing and transport infrastructure. However, this move was more of a nationalist gesture than the madcap challenge to capitalism envisaged by critics. The government recently signed a deal with Shell to develop oil and gas, while the huge Mutún iron reserves will be exploited in collaboration with the Indian company Jindal Steel and Power. This appeared unthinkable until recently, given

that ever since the conquest Bolivia has been stripped of its raw materials with little benefit to the native population. As we have seen, this was the main reason

behind the 2003 Gas War, and is a situation the populace is no longer prepared to accept.

Bolivia has suffered from the shortsightedness and egoism of its political, military, and business elite almost from the country's inception. It has been stripped of some commodities (gold, silver) and has sold others cheap in a succession of monocultures (guano, nitrates, tin). This exposure, rarely addressed by the country's leaders and compounded by the voracity of its neighbors, was often backed up by superpowers happy to use Bolivia as effectively a quarry for raw materials. Bilateral deals were struck with several European countries and South Africa, as well as South American neighbors. The full outcome of agreements with China to develop Bolivian energy resources has yet to be seen.

Bolivia and the Sea

An annual demonstration on March 23 reminds Bolivians of the crippling loss to Chile of their access to the sea in 1883. Eduardo Avaroa, the civilian who led resistance to the Chilean invasion, is revered as a national hero. Bolivia has made repeated attempts to regain at least a part of this coastline. The Chilean dictator Augusto Pinochet snubbed attempts by Hugo Banzer in 1975 and by Víctor Paz Estenssoro in 1988. The Peruvian president Alberto Fujimori offered the use of the port of Ilo to Jaime Paz Zamora in 1992, a populist but nonetheless useful gesture subsequently spurned by Bolivian governments, despite a road connection being built from Ilo to La Paz. There is currently hope for a new agreement with Chile.

Coca and Cocaine

The coca leaf, cultivated for centuries for medicinal and ritual uses in the Yungas north of La Paz, is a far more recent crop in the Chapare, near Cochabamba, where it is associated with the cocaine trade.

Drug trafficking has been a serious problem in Bolivia, leading to internal conflict and vehement resistance to legal measures imposed by the USA. The general mood of permissiveness toward this changed with the murder in 1986 of the naturalist Noel Kempff Mercado and two assistants, who accidentally landed on an airstrip used by *narcos* in the Huanchaca national park. Partly as a consequence, the National Congress passed Law 1,800, which drastically curtailed coca cultivation and encouraged alternative development, particularly in the Chapare.

The "Cocaine King," Beni landowner Roberto Suárez Gómez (1932–2000), whose great-uncle was the rubber baron Nicolás Suárez (see above), saw a business opportunity: instead of selling coca paste to Colombia for processing, he could develop the final product himself. Such was his success that he could buy off politicians and the military, famously once offering to pay Bolivia's foreign debt out of his own pocket. Suárez Gómez fell from grace in the late 1980s, with the return of civilian rule, and served seven years of a fifteen-year sentence. His story exemplifies the importance of the drug trade in the political process in Bolivia and elsewhere.

chapter two

VALUES &
ATTITUDES

FAMILY

The importance of the family in Bolivia, and its
dominance of social life, might seem strange to
many Anglo-Saxons. Strong family ties have not
been as weakened by individualism as in Europe.
People often live with their parents well into
adulthood, partly for financial reasons: there is no
stigma attached to this as in the US or northern
Europe. It is not unknown for parents and
unmarried children to grow old together without
the offspring ever having "flown the nest."

While old people's homes are more common
than before, not many families can afford or are
inclined to make use of them. It is still frequent
for three or more generations to live together in
the same house. Grandparents remain lucid and
able-bodied far longer than in the West, and play
a role in babysitting and other tasks. Even in the
case of better-off families, they complement or
even supplant the role of the maid. This
situation is cohesive, permitting octogenarians
and young children to communicate, and
encouraging mutual understanding between

generations that working parents do not have time to cultivate.

Family businesses are widespread, particularly in rural areas. Even if sons and daughters do not follow their parents' footsteps or continue the business, they are still expected to contribute some of their time. The poor might send their children out to shine shoes. Those who beg on the street do so with the support of very small children—mothers can be heard sending their children after some "target" likely to give money, such as a gringo backpacker.

The Progenitor's Zeal

As elsewhere in Latin America, it's seen as desirable to have children—and several of them. If you don't have offspring, people may assume you can't and treat you with sympathy. Other interpretations are also possible: one middle-aged gentleman in Sucre, who told me he had six children and found out I had none, paused before saying in a deadpan-jocular tone: "*Usted debe ser muy perezoso*" (You must be very lazy)!

WHAT'S IN A NAME?

Traditional "good" family names such as Cajías, Siles, Campero, Ballivián, and Paz may still raise eyebrows when dropped into a conversation, even though they have lost something of their previous importance in the prerevolutionary era, when such families had huge wealth and influence. There are names that go even further back, sometimes as far as the conquest. These are referred to with disparaging humor by ordinary people as displaying *rancio abolengo* ("rancid" lineage, presumably through having been around too long) and their resonance is more symbolic than real. There are still people with such names—Argandoña (a silver-mine owner who had his own bank) and Urriolagoitia in La Paz, Arana and Urioste in Sucre, Bowles and Vaca Diez in Santa Cruz—but they no longer wield any great authority. There is real muscle, though, behind names like Suárez (big landowners in the Santa Cruz area, not elsewhere) and Marinkovic (factory owner, landowner, and an example of the powerful Croatian presence in the same city).

At the other end of the scale, indigenous families may change their names in order to sound more Western and thus have a better chance in the job market. This still happens today, in spite of the fact that there is now more pride in the indigenous heritage. An example is the Aymara surname Mamani, which is bizarrely altered to Maisman. Quispe, which is of both Aymara and Quechua origin, might be changed to Quisbert. Yet it is hard to agree entirely with the remark by José David Condori (who preferred to retain his Aymara surname) that

Bolivia is the only country that discriminates against its own people: there are certainly others in Latin America.

Many Indians with Hispanic surnames simply took them from the *hacienda* to which they were tied, or had them imposed by their masters.

The working class, or indigenous people seeking some form of reflected prestige, often take, adapt, or distort names from the rich and famous in the developed world. Leydy and Dayana are still not uncommon (the British princess was extremely popular in this part of the world!). The film *Braveheart* gave rise to "William Wallace" as a first name. Bruce Limachi is slightly more cryptic, a homage to the martial arts movie legend. Víctor Hugo is not uncommon: neither are Bismarck, Denger, and even Blitz. In contrast, some middle-class parents, and foreigners who have had children in Bolivia, display a preference for indigenous names: Wara (star, in Aymara), Tupac and Amaru (separate names, but both taken from the eighteenth-century Cuzco Indian rebel Tupac Amaru), and Sisa (after Bartolina Sisa, wife of the Bolivian Aymara revolutionary Tupac Katari: see above).

ETHNICITY, CLASS, AND "CASTE"
Race is an extremely vexed issue in Bolivia. The 1993 constitution enshrined a multicultural and pluriethnic state, but many people would argue

that full ethnic equality is still a long way off. The issue is further complicated by the fact that many people's idea of their ethnic background varies according to questions of social and economic status.

It is quite rare to find a Bolivian whom a European or North American would describe as white; however, many people here consider themselves as such. Old inferiority complexes die hard, and there is still a system of racial hierarchy that is today, finally, being confronted. Various commentators have compared Bolivia to South Africa, and suggested that the current process of change is akin to the end of apartheid.

Not even wealth and a rise in social status can guarantee "whiteness." Simón I. Patiño, the "Tin King," built a vast mining empire in the 1920s and became one of the ten richest men on earth. Patiño was despised as an upstart mestizo by rival magnates, from older families, who had made their money through a "nobler" metal, silver. But he had the effrontery to become far richer than these supposed aristocrats.

A small Afro-Bolivian population has lived mostly in the tropical Yungas, north of La Paz, since independence in the nineteenth century. They are said to have migrated from the mines of Potosí, though there is little proof of this. The Afro-Bolivians now live by cultivating coffee, coca, and other crops. They are few (their numbers have not been satisfactorily calculated) but proud of their heritage; they wear Aymara-style clothing and speak Spanish but their music, known as *saya*, is unique and entirely their own—perhaps the only link with their African origin. They even have a king, Bonifacio, said to be descended from a royal line in Senegal.

MACHISMO AND GENDER RELATIONS

It is still difficult for a woman to rise to a prominent position in Bolivia, though this is gradually changing. Men still enjoy higher status in heterosexual relationships, though as in most Latin American households, the home is seen as the woman's domain. Domestic violence is still an issue, particularly but not exclusively in the countryside.

For the group of writers, artists, and researchers Mujeres Creando (Women Creating), based in La Paz, this situation is a constant provocation and source of material. This group uses graffiti to challenge preconceptions, also staging media events and publishing books and articles. Its confrontational style does not always convince, however: there is a feeling that change is underway in any case . . .

Gay issues are another area in which Bolivia is undergoing change. In the cities, it is now possible for gay couples to at least exist without having to keep up false appearances. One openly transvestite group, known as Familia Galán (Galán translates as "heartthrob") and based in La Paz, openly publicize their own tendency and queer issues in general.

The frequent beauty contests, the use of young women to "decorate" TV shows, the presence

 of girls in supermarkets offering samples of new products: all are examples of an attitude to women that seems at best old-fashioned to a Westerner. On the other hand, Anglo-Saxon cultural preconceptions would seem puritanical, not to say hypocritical, to many Latin Americans. There is also a clear division between Santa Cruz, where the members of the local glamour-girl group Las Magníficas are unquestioningly admired, and La Paz, where they

are viewed with derision. The image of beauty queens was tarnished by the 2004 Miss Bolivia, a young woman from Santa Cruz who told an interviewer that her people, unlike those from the Andes, were "tall, white, and speak English."

SOLIDARITY AND SUPPORT

Solidarity between close friends is absolute—even in cases where someone is demonstrably wrong or mistaken, their friends will support them (perhaps with a gentle admonition). People are also generous on a broader, national, or regional level: this was visible in the level of support offered during the flooding of the lowland departments in 2007 and 2008.

The Andean tradition of reciprocity gives rise to the concept of *ayni* (mutual support and cooperation, in Quechua). This is put into practice with the system of collective work known as *minka*, through which local people will help a neighbor with some particularly labor-intensive task. People in the countryside enjoy greeting strangers with a symbolic interchange of gifts; they may offer food or drink before asking for money. This should not be viewed as trickery or bad faith; cash is as hard to come by in the countryside as provisions can be for the visitor, and this is a reminder of *ayni*.

The *preste* is a particularly Bolivian phenomenon: according to this custom, the responsibility for funding an annual celebration falls each year on a particular member of a given group (whether professional, neighborhood, village, etc.). If nominated as *preste*, the person concerned will benefit in terms of prestige and status in the community concerned. Although the financial cost can be ruinous, shirking the burden would mean a serious loss of face.

WORK ETHIC AND ATTITUDES TO TIME

Jobs are not always easy to come by, and people tend to hang on to them, particularly in clerical or bureaucratic positions. Pay and other incentives are not sufficient to produce a sense of initiative, and workers will do just enough to stay in place without feeling any great involvement in their job or sense of belonging. This can be seen in various situations: for example, zealous policing is very rare, unless there are bribes involved. Customer service often leaves a lot to be desired, even in large companies. The customer is not always right in Bolivia: shopkeepers will rarely exert themselves, and may tell a potential customer an item is not in stock, even when it is clearly visible on the shelf behind them! Market vendors are often reluctant to sell off everything they have in one go: what else are they to do for the rest of the day?

There is little sense of the value (economic or otherwise) of other people's time, or guilt at keeping people waiting. A latecomer might explain: "I wasn't able to arrive early." "Early" is obviously an interpretation of "punctually."

ATTITUDES TO FOREIGNERS

Foreigners are treated with genuine interest and sincere hospitality, though there is undoubtedly an undercurrent of the kind of insecurity described in the "ethnicity" section above.

Many Bolivians have lived and worked abroad, or have relatives who do so in Europe, the United States, and other countries from which they send remittances. Those who remain in Bolivia often feel they have a certain familiarity with the country concerned, and are happy to strike up a conversation with visitors from that region.

Argentines are treated with a mixture of admiration and dislike. There are countless jokes about their supposedly huge egos, particularly people from Buenos Aires (a view by no means held only by Bolivians!). They are admired, however grudgingly, for their looks, their prowess at football (soccer) and in the arts, and other such attributes. Another recent factor influencing how Argentina is viewed is the number of Bolivians living there as migrant workers and subject to exploitation, often violence. The 2001 film *Bolivia*, by Adrián Caetano, deals with the not untypical fate of a Bolivian living in Buenos Aires.

There is also an ambiguous attitude toward other neighbors. Ordinary Chileans are not blamed for their government's expansionist policies, which, as we have seen, left Bolivia without a sea outlet. Bolivians generally like Chileans as people but still see them as eternal plagiarists who compensate for their lack of an original culture by appropriating others' inventions: for example, the Peruvian drink *pisco*, and the Bolivian dances *cueca*, *diablada*, and *caporales*.

Peruvians tend to get a bad press in Bolivia: at any sign of organized crime, Bolivians tend to assume that Peruvians have crossed the border to perpetrate it (though this assumption has recently been extended to include Chileans). Paraguayans are rarely encountered, but in any case are not frowned upon; the Chaco War is a distant memory. Brazilians are generally well regarded, though their country's incursions into unguarded Bolivian territory in past years mean that Brazil is not entirely trusted.

People from the United States are welcome, whatever the perception of their government's foreign policy. Britain has wronged Bolivia on numerous occasions, particularly through its support for Chile, but this seems to have been forgotten. People may even express regret that their country was conquered by Spain and not Britain! Many Brits will greet this sentiment with skepticism: what it does indicate is a lack of reverence for the Iberian "Motherland." The German presence in Bolivia has been varied (Nazi war criminals yesterday, generous development schemes today) but German nationals are well received, as are the other regular European visitors with active aid programs and a cultural presence: French, Italians, and Dutch.

REGIONALISM

Regional divisions are one of the most difficult problems Bolivia still has to resolve: today, they are complicated still further by issues of race and social class. Interregional prejudice is not confined to this country, of course, but it does have a particularly debilitating effect on a vulnerable land with such a small and unevenly distributed population.

People in La Paz (*paceños*) tend to speak ill of *cochabambinos* (from Cochabamba), who in turn berate *chuquisaqueños* (from Chuquisaca, whose capital is Sucre). Nobody is particularly keen on *paceños*. The rivalry between *collas* (Andeans) and *cambas* (inhabitants of the Oriente) has, in recent years, been stoked by the media and private interests into something far worse. It is now all but certain that the September 2008 "Porvenir massacre" was financed by wealthy landowners desperate to derail the government's project at all costs. Ex-prefect Leopoldo Fernández and other suspects are, at the time of writing, being arrested and are awaiting trial.

ATTITUDES TO THE LAW

Attitudes toward the law in Bolivia are largely informed by bravado and machismo: Bolivians see anything they are told to do by a higher authority as necessarily a pointless imposition. This attitude applies to traffic regulations and everything related to car ownership—formerly the preserve of the rich, who set themselves above the law. The payment of taxes is another area in which those who manage to fool the authorities are viewed with a certain admiration.

Recent moves toward institutionalizing "Community Justice" are one of the most interesting, if provocative, developments of the Morales era. This is a way of empowering indigenous communities and recognizing their authority and the validity of their values. It also lightens the load on the judiciary, whose implementation of "ordinary" justice might be resented by people in remote villages. Finally, the regime's acceptance of "judicial pluralism" is in keeping with the prevailing discourse of the times; it is proposed that decisions made under Community Justice should not be overturned or interfered with by "orthodox" courts. Thus the notion of hierarchy between town and country is avoided.

BUREAUCRACY

Bolivian bureaucracy is not as fearsome as one might imagine. However, it is worth asking a local expert (*tramitador/tramitadora*; *trámite* means "red tape" in Spanish) to help. Foreigners living in Bolivia can usually recommend someone suitable who perhaps has worked in government offices, has the relevant contacts, and can get things done swiftly and painlessly. A good *tramitador/a* will not ask you to do anything illegal such as offering bribes.

chapter three

RELIGION, CUSTOMS, & TRADITIONS

ORGANIZED RELIGION

Religious freedom is accepted without question in Bolivia—even to the extent of permitting some pernicious practices among purportedly spiritual organizations. Religion has long provided a smoke screen for various kinds of activities, though as ever there have been groups genuinely disposed to improve the well-being of those in their charge.

Bolivia has been a majority-Catholic country ever since the Spanish conquest, but its largely syncretic Catholicism is heavily influenced by indigenous beliefs. More recently Protestants, Baha'is, and other religious groups have made some inroads. Bolivia is likely to become a secular state without an official religion; the Roman Catholic Church is concerned less with this than with the possible reduction of the importance of religion in education and other areas of public life.

Gone are the days when Bolivians would unquestioningly accept all Church dictates, though the Catholic Church still plays an important role. People will often pop into church at spare

moments, not only for mass. Belief in God does
not necessarily mean unthinking obedience to the
Church. Anticlericalism has long been part of
religious life in the Hispanic world. An exception,
the popularly well regarded Jesuits, have always
considered welfare in this life as well as the next.

However, there are other forces at work these
days. Indigenous religions are still important,
though ancestral beliefs largely tolerated by
Catholics are being eroded with far greater zeal by
evangelical churches that have found Bolivia to be
fertile ground, especially given the historical
resentment toward Catholicism and its association
with the Spanish conquest. As long ago as 1988
Pope John Paul II, on a visit to Bolivia, warned
bishops about the threat from evangelism.

Mennonites have settled mainly in the Chaco.
The Mormon Church has its headquarters in
Cochabamba, where it built a large temple in
2000. Seventh-day Adventists, Baptists, and

Pentecostals are also active in Bolivia, as is the controversial Florida-based evangelical group, New Tribes Mission.

Sects like that of the Rev. Sun Myung Moon have always exploited vulnerable, corrupt states in their expansionist policies. Moon's Unification Church entered Bolivia in the 1960s, taking advantage of the Cold War atmosphere to establish itself through links with figures of such dubious virtue as Klaus Barbie and those behind the "narco-coup" of 1980.

The Baha'i religion has been popular in Bolivia since the second half of the twentieth century. Today it is the country's third-most popular organized religion, appealing to many with its emphasis on global unity, and its rejection of discrimination on grounds of ethnicity, gender, or social background. The Nur University, with branches in Santa Cruz and La Paz, is organized and financed by the Baha'i, who are one of the few religious bodies operating in Bolivia not formally accused of involvement in nefarious practices of any kind.

SPIRITUAL TRADITIONS
Bolivia is a land with a remarkable range of spiritual traditions, only a small fraction of which are given formal expression. There is no church or temple at which pre-Columbian deities are openly worshipped: as anthropologists like Olivia Harris and Tristan Platt have demonstrated, Christian festivals are at the same time opportunities to

LLEGADA DE. V. DE. CANDELARIA

honor the *achachilas* and *wakas*, which, according to indigenous belief systems, are the entities that guarantee continued life and well-being.

Indigenous Worldview
There are no longer any pristine indigenous cultures, even in a country as remote as Bolivia and with such a proportionately large indigenous population. But nor have Western ways of seeing the world entirely taken hold. The indigenous worldview sees everything as alive: even rocks are sentient beings. The harmony between opposites is crucial to this way of seeing things. The Andean universe is divided into *hanan* and *hurin*, complementary halves of the universe according to pre-Columbian cosmology. This is a division into complementary opposites such as upper and lower, male and female, rather than notions of good and evil or value judgements. Consequently, Catholic teachings robbed traditional Andean

concepts of their duality: for example, the dimensions *Alaxpacha*, *Akapacha*, and *Mankapacha* (above, upon, and below the earth) were turned into the realm of celestial, earthly, and malignant beings with correspondingly fixed Christian moral properties instead of the Andean ambivalence and mutability.

Indigenous beliefs have permeated even the ostensibly skeptical world of the cities: one notable custom is to spill the first few drops of an alcoholic drink onto the ground as an offering to the earth mother, Pachamama; only then is it considered correct to drink. This brief ritual is still performed in many places, and not just by indigenous people. Also common are *ch'alla* rituals, in which alcoholic beverages are not only consumed but also sprinkled over the object to be blessed and protected. The performance of *ch'alla* is particularly important when inaugurating a new house, but it can apply to numerous other ventures. It may be seen, for

instance, on a bus journey from La Paz to the Yungas—a recently improved, but still dangerous road, with a vertiginous descent from the mountains into the valleys. The driver will stop at the *cumbre*, the highest point, before alighting with a bottle of alcohol that he will ceremoniously splash over the wheels.

The juncture and interaction of ecological zones (mountain, valley, and jungle) is of great importance in the Andes, since trade cements relationships between neighboring peoples and guarantees local economies. The mythical bear, or Jukumari, is one such link, moving between high mountains and valleys. In one tale he oversteps the boundaries between species, carries off a young woman, and has a child by her. When she escapes with the child and returns to her family, Jukumari is condemned to wander in search of her.

The Pachamama is of supreme importance in the Andean pantheon. The earth mother is the definitive life-giver and, as such, essentially benign, but she must be regularly and adequately propitiated—particularly in August, which according to the Aymara is the month in which the earth opens itself to be fertilized. Belief in the Pachamama has resisted evangelization and all attempts to get rid of idolatry.

Conopas and *illas* are small figures with magical properties, carved in stone, usually in the form of alpacas.

Waka is a term common to Aymara and Quechua (often inadequately translated as "sacred"), which refers to natural and topographical features or crafted objects endowed with divine characteristics. The *waka* is also important in the social and political life of the community, in which it plays an integral part. Shamans (*yatiri* in Aymara, *layka* in Quechua) are instrumental in this integration of the spiritual and the political.

Achachilas (in Aymara, *apus* in Quechua) are protective spirits inhabiting and represented by the mountains, and linked to the ancestral past. "Payments" are made to the *achachilas* in the form of offerings and orations.

Malignant and Ambivalent Beings
A belief in zombies and imps of various kinds has long been part of Andean and other Bolivian lore. The *kari kari* (also known as *kharisiri*, *mikhala*, *condenado*, or condemned man) is one example. These are creatures that have departed from human existence without making their peace with the world, and still have some unpaid debt or unfinished task.

Sajras are spirits that emerge from underground: regarded as demonic in the Catholic scheme of things, they were nevertheless originally ambivalent creatures.

The *japiñuñu* (Quechua for "breasts that trap") appears as a beautiful naked woman who waylays lone travelers at night and suffocates them between her breasts.

These beings are not confined to the Andean world: in Chiquitanía, a belief in the *jichi* is a further example. The malevolent *jichi* makes a whistling sound as it flies about looking for mischief.

Some of these beliefs are clearly of Spanish origin. In the Chaco, the *salamanca* is a mythical dance of the devils in the depths of the forest. Stories of this spectacle were invented and endlessly elaborated by the settlers and migrant workers who traveled to cut sugar cane or pick cotton; they were used to frighten and discipline children or reinforce moral values.

There are numerous tales of sirens who inhabit the Bolivian rain forest and appear to lure credulous and unsuspecting men to their doom. In Homero Carvalho's short story *Nights of Desire*, the victim is a hapless rubber worker, enticed by unscrupulous employers into the jungle and bewitched by the siren, from whom not even his best friend can save him (see Further Reading: Richards 2004).

The Tío

The dangers involved in mine work, the sense of invading a space alien to normal human activity, led to belief in the Tío, implacable ruler of the underworld and godlike in his ability to decide over human life and death. The word ("uncle" in Spanish) may be a corruption of *dios* (god)— though certainly not in the strictly Christian sense; the Tío is represented in demonic form, inspiring fear and respect.

Before entering the mine shaft, miners make offerings to the Tío's effigy at every mine entrance. They light cigarettes and place them between the deity's lips; hard liquor is poured down his throat. Failure to observe these rituals might result in the Tío claiming the offender as part of the cull of miners that is his right. On the other hand, careful adherence to the rites could make one fabulously wealthy.

Superstitions
Superstitions are similar to those in Europe and North America: Bolivians are wary of black cats, ladders, and the number thirteen. Though some beliefs can be attributed to the natural environment, others are harder to explain. In some parts of the countryside, Monday and Friday are believed to be bad days for sowing crops; Thursday is generally a better day for launching any enterprise.

A *thaparanku* (big black moth) is a sign of impending death in the family, as is the sight of a dog digging the earth. On the other hand, a hummingbird augurs wealth.

FESTIVALS AND HOLIDAYS
There is a bewildering array of festivals in Bolivia: at any given time you are likely to be caught up in one

unexpectedly (see page 105). La Paz, for example, has some five hundred folk dances—one for every neighborhood in addition to its saint's day. These festivals inevitably involve brass bands, dancing, and considerable amounts of liquid refreshment. The use of alcohol, which might appear excessive to

outsiders, plays an important ritual role.

Space does not allow a full description of all the musical instruments, masks, and dress, to say nothing of the ritual complexity and significance of these many events. Below are some of the best-known and most interesting festivals.

Alasitas (La Paz: begins January 24)
This is one of Bolivia's most fascinating festivals. It isn't a pilgrimage, or a truly spiritual event, more an encounter between materialism and animism. A section of La Paz is given over to labyrinths of market stalls selling miniature versions of every kind of physical object the customer might desire. People simply buy tiny versions of what they want, have them "blessed" by one of the local shamans at the festival, and wait for the real thing to materialize. The power

being invoked by the shamans is threefold: the *achachilas*, the Pachamama (see above for both of these), and the dead—who are influential and often consulted for auguries and advice.

The most common figure in *Alasitas* is the *ekeko*, a small, laughing, rotund figure hung with banknotes, airline tickets, and other manifestations of material wealth—a representation of abundance derived from the ancient god of thunder, Thunupa. *Ekeko* figures are made for all budgets, some mass-produced in plaster, others crafted in silver.

Alasitas miniatures have a connection with indigenous *illas* (amulets) and *mullus* (small sculptures), which bring luck, wealth, and well-being; they reflect the native belief that objects contain an immanent spirit.

The merchandise can range from the humblest (building tools or kitchen instruments) to the most expensive (houses, jeeps) and even the stuff of intangible dreams and ambitions (miniature degree certificates, even Oscar statuettes!). Many people will swear to the effectiveness of *Alasitas* purchases in making dreams come true. Care should be taken with the banknotes on sale: you're advised to buy only the miniatures. However obviously fake they may be, it's not unknown for people carrying full-size *Alasitas* dollars to be arrested on arrival in the USA.

Carnival (throughout Bolivia: February)
There are numerous variations, but by far the
most famous is that of Oruro (page 79, below).

Fiesta de la Uva (**Grape Festival**) (Tarija:
March—the date varies)
A celebration of the vine and its by-products,
wine and *singani* (grape brandy).

Pujllay (Tarabuco, near Sucre: March 12–18)
The word *pujllay* means "play" in Quechua and is
applied to an indigenous dance and festival that
marks a military victory over the Spanish in 1816.
The festival brings together people from some
seventy communities in the region.

The so-called *Chope Fiesta* (**Great Festival**)
(Trinidad: May 25)
This is a celebration of the Holy Trinity, marking
the foundation of this tropical city. The

surrounding indigenous population comes to perform many traditional dances like the *machetero*, which is emblematic of the region.

Festival of Baroque Music (Chiquitos: last week of April to first week of May: dates vary)
This annual event marks the heritage of cooperation between indigenous people and Jesuits in the famous missions.

San Juan (throughout Bolivia: June 21)
Another syncretic celebration: the winter solstice has been made to coincide with the saint's day. It used to be marked by numerous bonfires, a practice recently curbed by the authorities because of its effect on air quality. *Campesinos* dedicate the festival to the well-being of their animals, burying *conopas* and *illas* (sacred objects in animal form, usually carved in stone) in corrals and sewing decorations to the ears of llamas.

Semana Santa (Holy Week: throughout Bolivia)
This is the major religious festival across Latin America. Pilgrimages such as the one from La Paz to Copacabana are still widely undertaken.

Gran Poder (La Paz: early June)
This festival began in the late 1930s in the working-class La Paz neighborhood of Chijini and has gained in importance ever since. Its adoption by the Church resulted from pressure exerted by the local

THREE IMPORTANT VIRGINS

• The Virgen de Copacabana, patron of
  Bolivia, is worshipped during a pilgrimage

on August 5. Her
famous image in
the Basilica of
Copacabana was
sculpted by one
of the pioneers
of religious
syncretism, Tito
Yupanki, in the
late sixteenth
century.
Copacabana, on
the shores of Lake
Titicaca, was a sacred site in pre-Columbian
times. The name is derived from the Aymara
deity Copacawana. It was later adopted for
the famous beach district of Rio de Janeiro.

• The Virgen de Cotoca is found in a village
  near Santa Cruz. Her feast days are
  December 8 and 15.

• The Virgen de Urkuphiña (Quillacollo, near
  Cochabamba: August 14–16). Three days of
  dancing and revelry to celebrate one of the
  legendary Virgins said to have appeared to
  indigenous people and worked miracles.

populace to accept its peculiar iconography, a Christ
with Three Faces painted with mestizo features that
graphically interprets the idea of the Holy Trinity.

Ch'utillos (Potosí: August)
Merged with the festival of Saint Bartholomew, this
is another pagan festival given a Christian veneer.
The festival was declared part of the National
Cultural Patrimony in 2005.

Todos Santos y Día de Los Muertos (**All Saints and
the Day of the Dead**) (throughout: November 1–2)
People flock to cemeteries to share with dead
relatives the things they loved when alive. This
festival, a combination of ancestral Andean rites with
the Christian festival of All Saints, has great
significance for ordinary people. The pre-Columbian
ceremony was *Ayamarqay Killa* during which the
dead were taken from their tombs (in which they
were placed in the fetal position) and carried in
procession. This is no longer held in its ancient form,
but aspects of it are still visible in some versions of
the celebration. Be prepared to pray for other
people's dead: your orations (in English if necessary)
will be "paid for" with fruit, sweets, and bread.

Ñañitas festival (cemeteries in El Alto and La Paz:
November 8)
A week later, people take out the skulls of their
dearly departed to be blessed by the priest. This is,
of course, an eminently pagan event, but the

faithful are charged an appreciable sum "per head" for the benediction. In 2008 the Church authorities decided to suspend the service, due to the pagan nature of the festival: this was greeted by sufficient outcry for it to be reinstated.

Ñañitas is an example of both the worshippers' syncretic adherence to their Andean traditions and pragmatism on the part of the Church. However macabre this may appear to the Westerner, it conveys a profound respect and veneration for the dead that is also linked to the life cycle and fertility.

Jisk'a Anata (La Paz: Thursday before Carnival) This is more intimate than Carnival and very recent. Since 1995 it has showcased examples of indigenous dance and music that might otherwise disappear. Groups gather from all corners of the country: their route can vary, so check in advance.

CARNIVAL IN ORURO

While the Rio carnival is known for its sensuality, abandon, and huge expense, what makes Oruro unique is the peculiar link between Christianity and indigenous cosmology, expressed in a range of dances and rituals that reflect the area's history and demographics. Oruro owes its sixteenth-century foundation to the nearby discovery of silver; great deposits of tin and other metals were later found in the nineteenth century. This meant mass migration for many farmers eager for the higher income available in the mines. It also involved the creation of new mythologies and belief systems appropriate to this new reality.

CARNIVAL DANCES

Carnival dances emphasize the coming together of peoples and creatures from all kinds of cultures and realms of being. Considerable sums are invested in the costumes, and great prestige can be gained through taking part. Dancers are organized into *comparsas*: these are groupings of various kinds; some are simply based on friendship, others are neighborhood, guild, or student groups. They are constantly being set up or disbanded, though some have lasted as long as fifty years. There is often a division along class lines, as more middle-class people seek the kudos of involvement.

The *diablada* is the central dance, a mass

movement of "devils" of dual origin. The Christian version, Satan or Lucifer, is merged with the indigenous mountain spirit Supay.

China Supay is the wife of Supay (*china* in Quechua means female). She emerges from the ranks of devils wearing a mask with huge blue eyes, sensuously curved horns, and a coquettish smile. She is the seductress, tempting the Archangel Gabriel who must resist as best he can. The nature of the dance has changed: China Supay formerly wore a repulsive devil's mask and was impersonated by male dancers. The Archangel Gabriel was once multiple, but now there is only one: apparently more dancers than ever before want to be devils.

The *morenada* represents the African slaves used in colonial times to drive indigenous mine workers. Its central figure is the *Rey Moreno* (King of the Blacks). Stylized masks emphasize the Africans' features, which were unknown in Latin America at the time.

The *caporales*, of much more recent origin, involves foremen with whips—this time, mestizos and mulattos. This is the most popular dance among the better-off.

The *tinku* ("encounter" or "confluence" in Quechua) is a dance version of the annual ritual battle waged by the cosmological opposites *hanan* and *hurin* of Andean religion (see page 67) to ensure the Pachamama's continued goodwill.

Suri sicuris dancers wear incredible headdresses with canes radiating from the center like spokes in a wheel. These are decorated with feathers, a representation of the Andean ostrich, or *suri*.

Tobas are the Amazonian Indians also known as Chunchos, who used to dance scantily clad

(courageously, given the Oruro climate) but who are now represented with huge headdresses and colorful costumes.

The *llamerada* has llama herders, evoking the primordial and symbiotic relationship between humans and animals in the Andean world.

Various satires on the appearance and behavior of the white masters include the *waka tocoris*, who "ride" a stylized bull onto which dancers are strapped: it mocks the bullfight. The *palla-palla* dance also pokes fun at the whites' appearance, while the *doctorcitos* derides the lawyers and secretaries who served colonial interests.

The bear (*oso* in Spanish, *jukumari* in Quechua) is a kind of clown who makes the dancers laugh and encourages spectators to join in.

The condor costume is made using real wings—though from dead condors rather than hunted ones, because this bird is revered. Its indigenous association is with the ancestors and the souls of the departed: it is also an iconic national symbol and appears on the Bolivian flag.

OTHER TRADITIONAL AND MODERN DANCES

Apart from the dances associated with Carnival, many others are still common in Bolivia.

The *cueca* is a kind of courtship dance, performed by couples who face one another without touching; each dancer flourishes a white handkerchief.

The *takirari* is a circular dance (*ronda*), which, despite its Andean name, is popular in Santa Cruz.

Wayñu describes a hybrid song form and dance in the Andes. It is performed during the rainy season, and is important in the agricultural cycle.

The *saya* comes from the tropical Yungas north of La Paz, and has its origins in Africa. As we have seen, the small black population living in this area has its own distinct culture, and its music and dance are reminders of its African origin.

The *lambada* never really caught on in Bolivia, but it originated in this country with the song *Llorando se fue* ("She left in tears") written by the brothers Ulises and Gonzalo Hermosa and recorded in 1983 by the popular group Los Kjarkas. The song was plagiarized by the Brazilian group Kaoma: the Bolivians accepted a settlement of US $1 million, a paltry sum considering its global success as emblematic of the dance craze.

The *cumbia* is a popular dance that originated in Colombia. Now somewhat electronically adulterated as *tecnocumbia*, it is all too often heard in minibuses and taxis.

chapter four

MAKING FRIENDS

FRIENDSHIP IN BOLIVIA

It is never difficult to make acquaintances in Bolivia; people are renowned for their extremely helpful and friendly nature, and are rightly proud of this reputation. However, genuine friendship, as anywhere else, is more elusive and takes time. Shared interests and a common outlook may help, but what probably distinguishes a real friend from an acquaintance is a readiness to give a frank and sincere opinion—most Bolivians would rather say what they think their interlocutor wants to hear.

Outsiders will find that the behavior toward them varies from region to region. Immediate

openness is rare in La Paz and the Altiplano, where people are more guarded until their respect and confidence have been won. Remember that these areas have seen rough treatment, directly or otherwise, at the hands of foreigners.

It may be a commonplace, but there is a correlation between human and climatic warmth. In tropical Santa Cruz people are far more immediately friendly and smile or talk more easily. A member of Che Guevara's clandestine guerrilla campaign in Santa Cruz was instructed never to walk twice down the same street; people would find out everything about her. *Cruceños* (natives of Santa Cruz) are naturally curious, and strongly believe that hospitality is a duty.

Bolivians do not form exclusive groups; if you are close to one person, it will be easy to get to know his or her friends. Cliques are the exception rather than the rule. Naturally friendships have to be worked at patiently, and national quirks taken on board. A "promise" to phone is anything but binding; do not be offended if it isn't honored. Next time you run into the person you'll be greeted warmly, and there is nothing false about this; however exasperating you may find it, the individual will not consider he or she has anything to apologize for. A greeting on the street is usually followed by a brief token conversation, which may end abruptly. Don't take it as a "brush-off" but rather as someone (who may be in a hurry) carrying out a social obligation.

Bolivians appreciate an open, friendly demeanor, but not excessively so. A degree of evident self-esteem is required for them to take you seriously. At the same time, you should avoid appearing haughty.

Bolivians are often genuinely flattered by outsiders who show an interest in their country. If you are there for a specific task or project, they will be keen to hear about it. You'll make friends, or at least have the beginnings of a social life, among the people you work and study with. Otherwise it's possible to strike up conversations at gatherings of people with common interests— at public talks, cultural events, bars, and plazas. It is not unusual to see groups of foreigners (whether residents or not) mingling with Bolivians.

FIRST MEETINGS
Bolivians are generally more guarded than their Peruvian neighbors when it comes to conversing with outsiders. Visitors need not expect repetitive questions, however good-natured, about their country of origin. This reticence reflects Bolivia's lack of contact with the outside world, a factor that has created an image of an absurdly remote country with

inaccessible people that has begun to change only during recent decades. In the 1950s Peruvian literary critic Luis Alberto Sánchez described Bolivia's writers as "*encuevados*" (literally, confined to caves, but translatable as willfully isolated rather than primitive). If less exuberant and demonstrative than many Latin Americans, Bolivians are nonetheless fascinated by foreigners and ready to welcome them.

Bars and fiestas are good places to get to know people, though of course excessive alcohol consumption is a poor basis upon which to build friendships. But people are at their most open in these situations, and they are plentiful: in Bolivia, life is to be enjoyed, whatever the current economic and political circumstances.

You may have come to the country with the address of a friend or relative of a Bolivian you got to know well in Europe, the United States, or elsewhere. The person you visit will go out of their way to make you feel welcome, putting you up at their home if possible.

INVITATIONS HOME
Invitations to stay overnight are not infrequent among established friends. Friendships among Bolivians may begin at school and continue into adulthood, and friends will have access to the house almost as part of the family. Even in later

life, close friends may visit on a very frequent basis. In old age, the custom of inviting a close circle for tea and card games is deep-rooted.

If you are invited to visit someone's house, it is a sure sign that your friendship is entering a new phase. You can take along a cake or pastries if invited for tea; if it is a party, take a bottle of wine or *singani* (grape brandy). Bolivians don't have set rules or demands of this kind, and you'll be welcomed even if you show up empty-handed. Dress code is a matter of common sense: go along with what prevails in the social group or according to the situation, and don't be afraid to ask if in doubt.

TIMEKEEPING

You should not arrive at the exact time if invited to a private gathering; this will make your hosts uncomfortable, since they will probably still be getting ready. Show up at least half an hour after the agreed upon time— but don't leave it more than an hour as there may be nothing left on the table! If you're invited to a formal diplomatic or business meeting, however, be punctual.

If meeting in a neutral place most Bolivians will keep you waiting, so when making an appointment choose somewhere safe and comfortable—not on the street. It may help to insist upon *hora inglesa*

(English time, which for some reason epitomizes punctuality). But while many Bolivians will still observe *hora boliviana*—some thirty minutes to an hour after the time agreed upon—you should beware of doing the same because some Bolivians are scrupulous timekeepers. Ask, politely but firmly, whether or not the appointment time is *en punto* (on the dot).

Remember, too, that Bolivian cities are not always easy to negotiate; even local people can get caught in traffic jams, stuck behind unforeseen marches and demonstrations, and so on. Make sure you have their cell phone numbers, to avoid misunderstandings.

PERSONAL AND SOCIAL BEHAVIOR

Greetings in Bolivia are quite formal: a woman is usually kissed on the cheek. A certain "manliness" is conveyed between men with a firm handshake (firmer in the Oriente than in the Andes, where they are no less sincere). Congratulations between men (on birthdays or engagements, for example) are restrained; each holds the other's forearms in a stylized "embrace."

Every culture has its ritualized behavior and Bolivia is no exception: when drinking in a group, for instance, the conversation will be punctuated by someone calling "*salud*" (cheers) whereupon everyone will raise their glasses and drink. If you raise your glass alone, it will be tolerated, though someone will call "*salud*" on your behalf: it is best to follow the group at least until everyone has had a few drinks. Younger people in La Paz tend to laugh in unison at a given signal—someone indicates they're joking by making a "*yaaa!*" noise.

Between individuals, etiquette is quite rigorously observed: people will say "*buenos días*" (good morning or good day) or "*buenas tardes*" (good afternoon) even while they're struggling into a crowded minibus. People tend to ask permission when leaving someone's presence. However, general social behavior is almost unregulated: people throw trash in the street, honk car horns and leave car alarms to shriek endlessly, talk on cell phones in cinemas—all these are examples of the antisocial behavior that is gradually being addressed by local government.

EXPATRIATE ASSOCIATIONS
Groupings of foreign nationals are inclusive of locals, and provide a way of meeting Bolivians. There is a Scottish dance group in La Paz, for example, in which only two Scots are regular members (Bolivians, French, and English make up the numbers). Certain foreign embassies (French, Brazilian) open their doors once a year for national day, though this is by invitation only. Some embassies—notably those of France, Italy, and Germany—are very active culturally. The programs of the Alliance Française and Goethe

Institut are always worth checking. Another very
lively cultural institution is the Patiño
Foundation, a legacy of the "Tin King" Simón I.
Patiño (see the section on ethnicity above), which
has branches in Cochabamba (the magnate's
mansion, named Portales) and other major cities.

HUMOR AND CONVERSATION

Bolivian humor is difficult to categorize: it can
range from anecdotal and childish to
sophisticated. What makes people laugh
understandably varies: in the countryside it is
playful, slapstick behavior and name-calling, at
times ingenuous and amusing to the outsider. In
cities, political correctness is not a major
consideration, and people rarely "tone down"
their jokes to avoid giving offense. However, there
are examples of a more sophisticated popular
humor that has elements of social commentary.
The highly successful comedy theater group Tra-
La-La subverts stereotypes (gender, regional, etc.),
satirizing "Bolivian-ness" without alienating its
popular audience. Its main figure is the
henpecked Pocholo, who wears an apron and
struggles to please his domineering wife.

A FEMALE PERSPECTIVE

Things are changing with regard to gender roles,
but men are still usually expected to take the

initiative in relationships. The expectation of sexual encounters on dates is still a question of social class.

Sexuality is generally more open in the Oriente than in the relatively chilly Andes, where things are literally and figuratively under cover. Infidelity is hardly unknown in any region of the country, and casual or furtive sexual encounters are quite common. Women are far less likely to make verbal propositions (still seen as a male prerogative) though they can, of course, express interest by other means. Casual liaisons are not infrequent in dark public corners between people who have nowhere more secluded to go.

Bolivian women in particular covet foreign partners, and not just for financial reasons. They see European and North American men as offering a relationship that is free of the machismo of which many Bolivian women complain: infidelity to the point of having two or more families, irresponsibility, and hedonism. Yet it is not uncommon for foreign women to take up with Bolivian men, often from an indigenous background.

The telephone plays a large part in many relationships—a man's willingness to call at least once a day is seen as proof of his devotion.

Inevitably, climate has a lot to do with how sexually provocative

people are or are seen to be. Santa Cruz is said
to have the most beautiful women in Bolivia
(or anywhere else, if the *cruceños* are to be
believed), but it is also true that they spend more
time and money on their appearance (cosmetic
surgery, clothing, and the like) than elsewhere
in the country.

Things are not always what they seem, and
people do not always say the truth. For example,
it is fairly common these days for Bolivian
couples to cohabit without being married, yet
a foreigner will frequently be told that they
are not doing so.

chapter five

THE BOLIVIANS AT HOME

HOUSING

The determining factors in Bolivian housing are much the same as in other areas of daily life: the geographical region, with its particular climatic conditions, dictates building materials and design, whereas economic status (ethnicity or social class) influences a dwelling's size, sophistication, and degree of security. The urban–rural dichotomy affects the quality of services available.

To begin with the regional: Andean houses used to be built of adobe blocks with roofs of *ichu*, a long, tough Altiplano grass. Today bricks or prefabricated blocks are generally used, with corrugated iron for roofs. Altiplano housing, in particular, must contend with fierce sun, wind, and rain, and afford protection to animals as well as humans, which usually also means a surrounding wall. This traditional farmer's dwelling can still be seen in parts of El Alto, though apartment blocks are now the norm. People still perform *ch'alla* rituals (see the section on spiritual traditions in Chapter 3), including burying a llama fetus under the house to ensure well-being within.

Rural houses in the tropical lowlands are of lighter materials like bamboo or timber, raised off the ground for ventilation, with the space below used for storage or garage space. This is also a precaution against flooding.

Some houses in the countryside are still quite rudimentary, with dirt floors and no electricity or basic services. Radio is crucial in these remote areas: local stations provide information and cement political allegiances (more on this in Chapter 9). Recent migrants to the cities often live in precarious conditions, in areas at risk of flooding or subsidence due to the steep terrain.

Some dwellings perch on the edges of cliffs and ravines on the outskirts of La Paz, seeming to defy gravity— unfortunately, not always successfully.

At the other end of the scale, rich urban residential areas are of two kinds: the longer-established urban families often move out of old city-center houses, which are bought up and demolished or converted into commercial spaces, office buildings, or shopping malls. The center becomes neglected and deteriorates, while the nouveaux riches live outside town in opulent but tasteless mansions with armed guards.

Older-style communal housing, or *conventillos*, were extensive, usually two-story dwellings, walled off from the street with several patios offering tranquillity, playing space for children, fresh air, and sunshine. However, these are increasingly being demolished and replaced, especially on main

roads, with unsightly residential blocks (*edificios*). People like this form of housing because of its aura of modernity and added security, but it removes almost all sense of community. Middle-class children are often left in the private nurseries (*guarderías*) springing up in residential areas.

Housing is increasingly in the hands of commercial developers as cities grow and are transformed. An estimated 70 percent is owner occupied, while 15 percent is rented, and another 15 percent simply occupied free of charge. Families who own their houses often expand them to make room for growth: when their children marry and start their own families, extra floors are built. Such factors, added to the loophole whereby owners of unfinished buildings do not pay property tax, mean much of the urban landscape appears permanently incomplete. Besides this, architects seem to want the public to see only one side of their work: the façade may be quite elaborate, but the other three surfaces are left as naked brickwork and concrete without paint or plaster.

Homelessness is a problem in Bolivia. The Sin Techo Movement (MST; *sin techo* literally means "roofless") sometimes squats unused land belonging to big concerns in El Alto, where widespread poverty and the inclement climate make the issue particularly urgent. Teatro Trono (Throne Theater), founded in 1989 in the Ciudad Satélite neighborhood of El Alto, has homeless youngsters write and act in their own plays.

CHILDREN

Bolivia's birthrate is high, and infant mortality is steadily decreasing (152 deaths per 1,000 births in 1960; 49.09 in 2008). Child welfare is also being addressed: state institutions now provide a school breakfast of fruit, yogurt, and crackers.

Medical centers such as the Hospital de la Mujer in Miraflores, La Paz, and the Maternidad Percy Boland in Santa Cruz offer free maternity services. In the countryside, the provision is less sophisticated and there is still a tradition of local midwives.

Many children are obliged to work and contribute to the family income; in cities this often means shoe shining. Children sell a monthly paper to supplement their income—*Hormigón armado* ("Reinforced Concrete"), similar to Britain's *The Big Issue.*

Rural children also work with the family, but unlike city children they perform tasks in and

around the home—shepherding, sowing seeds, and so on. Poor children, as elsewhere, are vulnerable to exploitation, and have been known to be snatched for organized sex and organ trading.

Contraceptive methods include IUDs, pills, injections, and condoms; sterilization is not uncommon. Though abortion is against the law, there are apparently many illegal terminations, though it is impossible to know the exact numbers.

EDUCATION

Bolivia's leaders have rarely been prepared to implement an adequate education system. Bolivia used to have the lowest literacy rate in South America, but this has now changed: it has just been declared the third Latin American country to be free of illiteracy. The other two countries, Cuba and Venezuela, ran a campaign in Bolivia in 2006 using literacy techniques applied in Cuba in the 1960s. Even now there is much left to do.

While Bolivians recognize the importance of formal education, this is not yet universally and uniformly applied. Technically education is compulsory, but small children can always be seen performing menial tasks for a few pesos. A recent government scheme, the *Bono Juancito Pinto*, now offers cash incentives to poor families, replacing what children might earn on the street and effectively financing their education. The results of this measure have not yet been evaluated. The eternal male–female and urban–rural discrepancies apply here, too.

One important educational pioneer, Avelino Siñani, campaigned for an indigenous school in his native Warisata (near La Paz) in the early twentieth century, a time when landowners expressly forbade instruction for Indians. Siñani was beaten and imprisoned for his efforts, but prevailed: his success did not go unnoticed. Politicians courted him, for literacy meant the right to vote and recently educated Indians could swing the results of the elections. Siñani refused to be bought, but accepted offers of money to create further schools.

The 1952 Revolution brought substantial changes; before this, only an estimated one-third of the population was literate. From 1956 a six-year primary education cycle was introduced, followed by an intermediate period of four

years, and another four of secondary education terminating in the baccalaureate qualification. During the last two years, students are required to choose a specialization—in either humanities or one of numerous technical subjects.

The urban–rural gap is due in part to the elite not seeing the education of Indians as either worthwhile or politically safe. Parents often feel the same way about schooling for girls. Spanish is not always spoken in rural areas: bilingual education was instigated under the first Sánchez de Losada government, and has continued, often with foreign funding, with patchy results. There is still no academic consensus on Quechua and Aymara grammar and orthography.

As for higher education, thirty-five private universities have opened in the last twenty years, but students, usually from wealthy families, are often viewed as "clients" rather than pupils. They rarely fail, being under no great pressure to earn whatever qualification they obtain. Some private universities are now offering places to the rural poor; whether out of a genuine desire to improve access to education or due to political opportunism remains to be seen.

There are only ten state universities, in La Paz, Sucre, Cochabamba, Santa Cruz, and Oruro. They are available to all sectors of society and charge nominal fees: unlike the private institutions there is some rigor and integrity when it comes to grading.

MILITARY SERVICE

Military service is obligatory for males over eighteen, though in any crisis deemed a national emergency the government reserves the right to call on boys as young as fourteen. In *campesino* families, military service is still seen as a way for young men to prove themselves. Middle-class parents are more likely to see it as an obstacle to education and a career: in fact, service can be postponed if the individual has already enrolled at a university. Once a university qualification is obtained, then professional "assimilation" to the military ensues, with the rank of sublieutenant, for one year. Exemption is allowed in the case of physical or mental disability.

Today there is an increasing awareness of a conscript's right not to submit to humiliating and degrading treatment. A recent case promises to be exemplary: a sergeant was arrested in August 2008 for allegedly beating a nineteen-year-old conscript to death. This kind of abuse, with impunity for the perpetrators, has long been tolerated in Bolivia.

The abolition of compulsory military service, and its replacement by voluntary service and a professional army, has been under discussion recently. Former conscripts have been pressing for change and for guilty officers to be brought to trial.

MARRIAGE

On Saturdays cars can be seen dragging strings of tin cans around La Paz and other cities, emblazoned with

wedding messages: the couple visit places
they wish to frequent in married life.
These couples, of Indian origin but used
to city life, can be seen walking through El
Alto airport and across the spectacular Bridge of the
Americas, still sprinkled with rice or confetti.

Such rituals may or may not be accompanied by
a religious ceremony because a church wedding is
not obligatory in Bolivia; in fact, only a civil
wedding is legally valid. A church ceremony,
however, especially a Catholic one, may be seen as
socially and morally superior: even people who
have converted to evangelical Christianity are
known to prefer Catholic ceremonies because they
are more impressive.

The legal minimum age for men to marry is
sixteen; for women it is fourteen if they have their
parents' permission. In Andean indigenous
communities, where a woman's virginity is not
considered a part of her "value," couples will enter
into what is known as *sirwiñaku*, a period of trial
marriage. This convention is entirely respected by
the community and is in no way tainted with
Christian notions of sin. If the two get along well,
then they have time to save up for the substantial
expense of a wedding, with its attendant fiesta.

WORK AND THE DAILY ROUND

Bolivians tend to work (or at least occupy their
place of work) for long hours. The working day

usually begins at 9:00 a.m. for office workers and ends around 7:00 p.m. The main meal of the day is generally lunch: a two- to three-hour break means the whole family can gather for this, and there is siesta time for it to be digested afterward. Alternatively, people may go out to lunch at a nearby restaurant, bring their own food, or even work through the day in some cases. This means the average day is cut into two, and working hours stretch into the evening—something that non-Latin Americans find hard to get used to. Whenever there is a shorter working day, or an impending public holiday, the boss will declare *hora continua*, meaning that workers will not take a lunch break but instead will leave considerably earlier than usual.

People shop daily at the many street markets, though supermarkets are becoming more common and sometimes undercut the opposition for fruit and vegetables.

The night hours are usually spent on the street in the warmer regions, sitting Mediterranean-style in doorways or plazas. However, even on cooler nights in La Paz young people often gather outside for a drink (from a bottle: cheaper than going to a bar!).

TIME OUT

Bolivians are sociable, gregarious people who enjoy their leisure time to the full to make up for the effort involved in day-to-day survival. Not many people can get by with just one job or activity; even for those who can, they usually have to work long hours. Leisure is enjoyed passionately and there are many opportunities; compared to most people in the "developed" world, Bolivians have a great deal of free time. Local people make sure outsiders feel welcome, and you need have no hesitation about showing up at festivities of any kind.

NATIONAL PUBLIC HOLIDAYS (*FERIADOS*)

New Year's Day	January 1
Carnival	February (movable)
Good Friday	March/April (movable)
Labor Day	May 1
Corpus Christi:	July 11
National Day	August 6
All Saints	November 1
Day of the Dead	November 2
Christmas Eve (more celebrated than Christmas Day)	December 24
Christmas Day	December 25

Local and regional public holidays celebrate memorable dates. July 16 in La Paz, for instance, commemorates the date (in 1809) of the first movement toward independence. There may be variations and exceptions, with holidays moved to the first or last working days of the week, so it's best to check before traveling within the country.

OTHER DEPARTMENTAL HOLIDAYS

Beni	November 18
Chuquisaca	May 25
Cochabamba	September 14
Oruro	February 10
Pando	October 1
Potosí	November 10
Santa Cruz	September 24
Tarija	April 15

State employees in Bolivia have one month's paid holiday, half of which is taken in winter (mid-June to mid-July in the southern hemisphere) and the rest either side of New Year. The same should also apply to those employed by private companies, but it is not always respected.

Not many Bolivians are able to take what would be considered a vacation by people in the developed world, at least on what they themselves earn; travel abroad is expensive, especially by air. Most working people will take vacations within Bolivia, perhaps visiting some spot in the countryside. People with relatives in other parts of the country might pay them a visit. Those with relatives in neighboring countries, the United States, or Europe may even be sent money to cover the trip.

EATING AND DRINKING

A popular belief in Bolivia is that, however severe the poverty, people don't starve. It is certainly true that the country produces a great deal of food, of considerable variety and quality. Bolivia is still primarily an agrarian country, but exports little of its produce due to the lack of a decent transport infrastructure.

Bolivian cuisine varies greatly from one region to another. In the Andes the staple is, of course, the indigenous potato—there are hundreds of excellent varieties, of which some fifteen are generally

available. One Andean specialty is black *chuño*,
naturally freeze-dried in alternate sun and frost.
A white variety, *tunta*, is produced by a different
process. An acquired taste, but they feature in
many Andean Creole dishes. Many middle-class
people mystifyingly prefer the greatly inferior rice
or pasta on offer.

Cities at a high altitude like La Paz, Oruro, and
Potosí enjoy produce from the Altiplano
including llama meat, nutritious grains such as
quinua, *kiwicha*, and *cañahua*, and tubers like *oca*
and *olluca*. They are also provided with fruits of
all kinds from the temperate valleys. Fruit familiar
to Europeans and North Americans such as
apples, pears, and strawberries are all available,
but more exotic and delicious items are also easily
found: mango, papaya, *tumbo* (a tropical fruit
used for juice), and many others.

Cochabamba is in the main agricultural area
of the Andean valleys and one of the country's

foremost culinary centers. This is probably the best place in Bolivia to eat. It is said of *cochabambinos* that their greatest pleasure in life is eating, something borne out by the fact that they have no fewer than five mealtimes! A dish served at around 10:00 a.m. bridges the gap between breakfast and lunch, while another at 4:00 p.m. eases the wait until dinner. All the same, cases of obesity are quite rare in Cochabamba.

Santa Cruz is now a major soybean producer, a development that has brought economic success but raised environmental concerns: it also means soybean oil is plentiful. However, even this can become a political weapon; in 2008 there was a standoff between producers seeking higher prices abroad and the government that suspended exports and capped prices. Other foodstuffs produced in the area are sugarcane, rice, vanilla, coffee, sunflower seed and oil, cacao, various green vegetables, and citrus and tropical fruits.

A Selection of Bolivian Dishes
Chairo An excellent and nutritious vegetable soup, originally from La Paz. It contains *chuño*, broad and long beans, potato and onion, and often but not always beef and lamb.

Lawa Another type of Andean soup that, unlike *chairo*, is deliciously smooth (it is usually made with ground peanut, maize, or some other flour).

Ají de lengua Tongue cooked in spicy sauce: other meats can be prepared in this way, as well as pasta (ask for *ají de fideo*, a spicy pasta).

Sajta de pollo A mouthwatering chicken dish cooked with **chuño phuti** (*chuño* with egg, finely chopped onion, and tomato) as well as potato, ground yellow pepper, and other vegetables. A cold Bolivian beer is the perfect accompaniment.

Pique macho (Cochabamba) Usually served in gargantuan portions, a dish of potato, beef, and vegetables all chopped and attractively arranged on the plate. Like many successful dishes, this one was supposedly born of adversity: a hostess faced with an unexpected surge of guests had to satisfy them by stretching a limited amount of food, and did so by chopping up all her ingredients—thus creating the illusion of plenty. However, the size of today's portions in Cochabamba is no longer illusory!

Pastries There are a number of delicious pastries from the Santa Cruz area, made from yucca (*sonso*), maize (*bizcocho*), and green plantain (*masaco*).

Fish A notable absence from Bolivian cuisine is fresh seafood. But there is excellent freshwater fish: trout from Lake Titicaca and a tiny Altiplano fish called *ispi*, delicious fried and served with lemon juice. From lowland rivers and lakes comes *surubí*, a large fish served as steaks, and others such as *sábalo* and *pacú*, served fried or grilled; they are fresh in the Oriente but also available (frozen, but still acceptable) in the Andean cities.

Drinks

Api A delicious hot drink made from ground maize (either yellow or purple) with cloves and cinnamon, usually accompanied by fried pastries containing cheese. Ideal for keeping out the Altiplano chill.

Mokochinchi A refreshing soft peach drink (a dried fruit is contained in every glass).

Tea Residual British influence can be seen in the habit of taking tea at 5:00 p.m.—even if this custom is rarely observed in the UK today. Other infusions are known as *mate*: they can be chamomile, aniseed, dried fruits, and others. The version of *mate* popular in Argentina, Uruguay, and Paraguay, prepared in gourds and drunk through a metal tube, is also consumed in the Chaco and other areas of Bolivia.

Coffee The welcome proliferation of coffee bars in the bigger cities since the late 1990s means that it is no longer impossible to find a good cup of coffee.

Wines The best South American wines are beyond doubt from Argentina and Chile, but Bolivia's Concepción, from the Concepción valley near Tarija, invites comparison with any of them.

Singani This is a grape brandy, not unlike the Peruvian *pisco* but based on the Alejandría muscatel grape, used in popular drinks such as *yungueñito* (*singani* with ice and orange juice).

Beer Bolivian beer is very good indeed thanks to the breweries set up by Germans, particularly in La Paz and Oruro.

Chicha A traditional Andean drink made from fermented maize that is popular throughout the region, especially in Bolivia and Peru. Bolivia's best and most prolific area for *chicha* is Cochabamba.

Apthapi A tradition that emphasizes the communal aspects of Aymara society. Everyone brings some food, which is laid out to be shared and eaten with the hands. It is a form of welcome, or a way of partaking of food during a group work project. The word *apthapi* is now used metaphorically for any event in which all participants contribute, ensuring variety and a shared experience.

Coca

This is one of the great bones of contention in Bolivia's external relations, especially with the US. The coca leaf, as is well-known, is not a narcotic: it has been used for medicinal purposes for millennia. While not exactly a food, it is often used as a substitute for eating. It removes hunger pangs, and can do the same with tiredness, cold, and altitude sickness, or *soroche* (coca-leaf tea can help). The visitor should not be surprised, especially in the countryside, to see people with one distended cheek stuffed with the leaf.

DINING OUT

In the main cities, a wide range of restaurants caters

to most diets, palates, and budgets. In tourist areas they soothe homesick gringos with eateries often run by French, Germans, Austrians, and Italians; there is even a "British curry house" in La Paz. There is also Chinese fare ("Chifa" in South America) as well as Japanese and Middle Eastern cuisine. McDonald's in La Paz soon closed through customer indifference: Burger King survives. Peruvian, Argentine, and Brazilian

food is available. National restaurants range from humble family premises to fast food places such as Pollos Copacabana (serving chicken). Of course, there are classier Bolivian restaurants serving a full range of national cuisine.

Vegetarian food is more easily available than ever, since there is a growing awareness of the dangers of excessive meat consumption. If you are a strict vegetarian, it is better to find an exclusively vegetarian place (or one of the national chains, which have set menus) rather than trust a "regular" restaurant to serve you a meat-free meal.

TIPPING

Do not wait to be seated in restaurants. It is customary, if discretionary, to leave a tip of 10 percent. Tipping is not usual in taxis and other situations except in recognition of particularly good service.

STREET AND MARKET STALLS

Many foreign residents have no problems to report after eating and drinking on Latin American streets—judiciously and with common sense, it should be added—for many years. Among Bolivia's delights are the fruit juice stalls at which a huge array of both tropical and more familiar fruits are blended and served in clean glasses. It's an excellent supplement to one's diet and a boon on hot days.

Other street fare are *salchipapas* (fried and chopped potato with sausage) and *papá rellena* (potato mashed, shaped, and stuffed with various fillings before being fried).

MONEY AND BANKING

The Bolivian peso, or Boliviano, has been quite a stable currency for some time now, a far cry from the rampant inflation of the mid-1980s, when piles of notes might be carried in wheelbarrows or measured with a ruler rather than counted.

In recent years the Boliviano has actually been climbing against the US dollar, a currency whose omnipotence in  Latin America is no longer taken for granted. When receiving dollars, it is important to check that they are not ripped: damaged bills may be refused, or changed at a lower rate.

The Euro is becoming more popular, and it's now possible to open a Euro bank account. Bolivia is one of the few Latin American countries where British pounds may be exchanged, but it is far more advisable to travel with dollars or Euros.

The cash card has made life in Latin America far easier, but see the warning under "*Secuestro Express*" in Chapter 7.

WHAT TO BUY

Consumerism has yet to take any great hold in Bolivia, and shopping malls are few. Instead, many consumer goods are imported or pirated, which makes them available to the average pocketbook. It is pleasant to stroll through the long stretches of market that still have a traditional feel to them in terms of human interaction, even if the wares are far from

traditional. Cochabamba's Cancha, Santa Cruz's
Siete Calles, and Uyustus in La Paz are markets
where everything is available from foodstuffs to
clothing to electronics. Municipal enclosed
markets are largely for comestibles, with eating
areas and juice stalls. They tend to be surrounded
by small stands selling gadgets and hardware,
giving a traditional feel, although those in Sucre
and La Paz are now housed in modern buildings.

The best place for a range of national arts and
crafts (indigenous weavings, silverwork, carvings,
paintings, etc.) is the area around the Calle
Sagárnaga in La Paz. Of course, if you travel to
where these crafts originate your experience
will be more exciting, and should result in better
prices. Bargaining is expected; otherwise you
will pay gringo rates. Be resolute, but pleasant;
you'll do better charming people than trying to
bully them.

ENTERTAINMENT

Carnivals and *feriados* (national public holidays) provide free entertainment, while the well-heeled urban youth gravitates to discotheques. Santa Cruz is acknowledged to have the best nightlife in Bolivia, with its barrages of discos in the Equipetrol district, considered superior to those in other cities.

For more traditional entertainment, there are numerous clubs for live music (*peñas*), where many types of music are on offer. The Andean folk music heard at such places is of the "sanitized" kind, removed from its original rural context for tourists and urban Bolivians. The type of romantic ballad known as the *bolero* is still popular among the middle-aged. Jazz clubs such as  Thelonius in Sopocachi (La Paz) are frequented by urban middle-class Bolivians and foreigners.

Dances with live *cumbia* (see Chapter 3) are popular among younger audiences, while local rock bands play in cities: Rap is performed in El Alto, sometimes in Aymara. Older people like the traditional *cueca* dance music, or the romantic *bolero*. All this music can be found either at free events or paying concerts.

LITERATURE AND FILM

Because of the generally low level of adult literacy, the audience for creative literature in Bolivia is very small. Reading fiction or poetry is mostly confined to a middle-class minority. Bolivia's isolation has meant that its writers have rarely found a readership abroad, while lack of funding has seriously shackled filmmakers. Nonetheless there have been notable exponents of both arts. The highly distinctive La Paz poet and narrator Jaime Saenz (1921–86), probably the best-known Bolivian writer, is widely translated and published in English.

Cinema-going, however, is making a comeback in Bolivia, thanks partly to the multiscreen centers opening in the main cities. Most casual spectators still prefer Hollywood movies, though there is a growing interest in national cinema. The nation's active and creative intelligentsia tends to frequent certain areas of the cities, with La Paz at its head, and inevitably produces art for a limited audience—though in the case of film, there is more possibility of reaching a broader public.

Jorge Sanjinés is the country's outstanding filmmaker to date. With his Ukamau group, he has made a series of radical films such as *La nación clandestina* (*The Clandestine Nation*, 1989) defending indigenous and workers' rights against the military dictatorships of the 1960s and 1970s. More recent Bolivian films are now available on DVD (legitimate copies, on whose sales filmmakers depend, are available from the Cinemateca in La Paz).

Other recommended films are Rodrigo Bellott's innovative social comedy *¿Quién mató a la llamita blanca?* (*Who Killed the Little White Llama?*, 2006; English subtitles) and Marcos Loayza's *Cuestión de fe* (*A Matter of Faith*, 1995; not subtitled). Antonio Eguino's historical drama *Los Andes no creen en Dios* (*The Andes do not Believe in God*, 2006) carefully reconstructs the early twentieth-century mining boom in Uyuni, and features a lovingly restored steam train in several scenes. Paolo Agazzi's popular films are also available, but without subtitles. Juan Carlos Valdivia's *American Visa* (2005) adapts Juan de Recacochea's novel tracing a provincial teacher's frustrated attempt to emigrate to the USA.

The opening of the new Cinemateca Boliviana (Bolivian Film Institute) in 2007 has brought a fillip to moviegoing in La Paz, as well as the Cine Centers in Cochabamba and Santa Cruz. Hopefully, these will restore a social habit that has suffered from television, the video recorder, and more recently the virtually unchecked boom in pirate DVDs.

OUTDOOR ACTIVITIES

There are plentiful hiking opportunities in Bolivia, particularly in the area to the north of La Paz. Do not confuse the Bolivian Camino del Inca (Inca Trail) with the Peruvian hike to Machu Picchu, but it offers spectacular views between La Paz and the warm valleys (the Yungas) hundreds of feet below. The walk is almost all downhill.

Other healthy pursuits that allow the Andean landscape to be enjoyed are cycling, backpacking, and climbing. In the subtropics and lowlands there are white-water rafting and canoeing.

Bolivians are not really given to such exertions, though some excellent local guides are to be found for these activities. People who live in remote mountain valleys often have little alternative but to walk. A day out for Bolivians often entails a trip to the nearest park, zoo, pool, or lake if there is one (more likely in the Oriente). Water-based activities are rarer in the Andes, though La Paz has some indoor pools.

Football (soccer) is almost the only sport that generates true passion throughout Bolivia. Unfortunately, the national side is rarely successful. It has only qualified once for the World Cup finals, in the USA in 1994, and though it performed honorably it was still eliminated at the group stage. Bolivia participated in the first World Cup (Uruguay, 1930) but by invitation; the results were ignominious. Bolivia chalked up one American Nations' championship (Copa América) as host nation in 1963, and was runner-up to Brazil, again as host, in 1997.

Bad news for Bolivia came in 2008, when, under pressure from Brazil, the international body FIFA finally banned World Cup qualifying and Copa Libertadores matches played above 2,500 meters (8,202 feet). This prevents Bolivia playing in La

Paz, in whose rarefied mountain air giants like
Brazil and Argentina have regularly faltered. (This
ban has yet to be implemented, however.)

The main rivalry among Bolivian football
teams is between the La Paz sides Bolívar and The
Strongest. However, on days when a derby match
(*clásico*) is played between these two there is never
any crowd trouble—people dressed in the black
and gold of The Strongest and the sky blue of
Bolívar can be seen walking side by side to and
from the stadium. Aurora and Jorge Wilstermann
in Cochabamba is another rivalry, as is Oriente
Petrolero and Blooming in Santa Cruz. The
closest a Bolivian club has come to a major
international trophy was when Bolívar was
runner-up in the 2004 Copa Sudamericana.

A more recent development is football between
cholas, who play in skirts and pull no punches as
regards tackling and other physical contact.
Cholas also have a wrestling (*cachascán*) league,
popular on Sundays in El Alto.

chapter seven

TRAVEL, HEALTH, & SAFETY

GETTING AROUND

Bolivia's transport companies are gradually falling into line with those in neighboring countries such as Chile, Argentina, and Brazil, where safety, comfort, and punctuality are the conveyor's responsibility to the passenger. However, Bolivia still faces severe infrastructure problems, as well as other difficulties (like roadblocks) related to the political situation. Interurban travel is improving; but reaching remote places remains difficult and at times grueling. Road travel is recommended for those travelers who wish to get a feel for the country and the everyday reality of its inhabitants. Bolivians will engage in conversation whenever their interlocutor's level of Spanish permits, and often the tougher, longer trips generate a sense of camaraderie and openness.

Distance and time do not necessarily correlate as in other countries, and the usual question is how long a journey takes, rather than how far the destination. The most honest reply is: we arrive when we get there; innumerable imponderables and contingencies can await the traveler.

Flying

Air travel is the safest mode of transport as well as the fastest, but it is still prohibitively expensive for most Bolivians. On a domestic flight you are more likely to be in the company of business people, tourists, and wealthy *cholas* from the Aymara merchant class.

Bolivia's state airline, Lloyd Aéreo Boliviano (LAB), is still reeling from the effects of the severe mismanagement that led to its suspension in April 2007. Service is still to be resumed; meanwhile most of the business has been handled by the country's biggest private carrier, AeroSur, which serves all the main cities. Flights mostly to smaller towns in Beni and Pando can be found with both Amaszonas and another tourist airline, Aerocon, which styles itself Beni's flagship airline.

Aeroeste operates out of Santa Cruz's smaller airport, El Trompillo, and mostly serves the oil industry. Be aware that there are two airlines named TAM, both offering cheap fares: TAM Mercosur serves various destinations in Bolivia, Argentina, Uruguay, and Brazil as well as its base, Paraguay. The Bolivian military carrier TAM (Transporte Aéreo Militar) is a source of income for the air force and also serves civilians.

Trains

Unfortunately, Bolivia's train services have been severely reduced by the road lobby.

The name "*Tren de la Muerte*" (Train of Death) is an example of Bolivian gallows humor applied to the long, hot, unpleasant, mosquito-infested trip between Santa Cruz and the Brazilian city of Corumbá.

In the west, trains link Oruro with the tourist destination of Uyuni and the Argentine border at Villazón. The Ferrobús passenger services from La Paz to Cochabamba, and from La Paz to Arica on the Chilean coast, are now sadly defunct.

The Madeira–Mamoré line through tropical border territory was built at considerable human and economic expense as part of Brazil's payment for the Acre territory. In 1972 it became economically unviable.

By Water
It should be remembered that, despite Bolivia's landlocked condition, the country still has a navy (operating on Lake Titicaca and the eastern river

systems) and a number of passenger services in both areas. Riverboats run along Bolivia's main waterways such as the Beni and Mamoré rivers, and the Pantanal system bordering Brazil. They are much less stressful and uncomfortable than traveling by road and are

much cheaper than flying. They also offer the
possibility of getting to know locals and seeing
wildlife.

Buses
Bolivia's overall road infrastructure has improved
considerably over the last fifteen years or so. Major
cities are now connected by tarmac roads, which
have replaced impacted surfaces. This means that
the constant noise
and vibration of a
bus journey are a
thing of the past.
However, technology
has replaced this with
the DVD: passengers
are at the mercy of
the average bus
crew's notion of what
makes a good film,

which usually entails generous helpings of
gunshots, yelling, and crunching of bones at
full volume.

All in all, intercity bus journeys are improving.
However, the more roads improve, the faster
people drive. There is currently a government
campaign to curb lunatic drivers, with checks
and passenger questionnaires to detect alcohol
consumption, overwork, and other factors.

Air-conditioning is available on some lines
but is not needed on highland routes such as La

Paz–Cochabamba. The quality of service (and degree of safety) offered by the various bus companies (*flotas*) varies. If possible, check with local people as to which is the best company.

Trucks are used in more remote areas, with rural passengers prepared to stand for hours, sometimes in the rain with no cover.

Urban Transportation
Getting around cities is relatively easy and inexpensive. La Paz has three types of public transportation. *Microbuses* are old Dodge school buses painted up both for aesthetic reasons and to distinguish the route. They are cheaper but slower than the *minibuses*, which are paradoxically smaller than the *micros*. People more than 6 feet (1.84 m) tall may find it extremely uncomfortable to get in and out of these conveyances. There is also the *TRUFI*, a taxi that travels a fixed route and can take up to five passengers (*TRUFI* is an acronym derived from **TR**ansporte **U**rbano de Ruta **FI**ja).

Taxis are plentiful: those without a lighted sign on the roof are cheaper but are entitled to take other passengers going the same way. The more expensive "Radio taxis" may only take one fare at a time: it is recommended you pay the extra and take one of these after dark because single passengers in standard taxis have become targets for thieves. Some people prefer to call known taxi companies from their own area by cell phone.

Other cities have their peculiarities when it comes to transportation: in Trinidad, like many low-lying tropical cities, motorbikes (*mototaxis*) predominate. Given the heat, this makes for a more pleasant ride; but the city sounds constantly like a freshly disturbed beehive.

Problems with noise and pollution are finally prompting local authorities to consider alternatives to motor vehicles. A raised monorail connecting the sprawling satellite city of El Alto, on the plain above, to La Paz and the wealthy suburb of Zona Sur in the canyon below has long been debated, but faces fierce opposition from the powerful bus-operators' lobby.

Bicitaxis (two-seater, three-wheeled bicycles) would be feasible in cities on flat terrain such as Santa Cruz, Oruro, and El Alto. They have already been introduced in some Peruvian cities and in Havana, Cuba.

Foreigners need to get used to the way Bolivians use the sidewalk: people tend to gather and talk, or just stand still, even on the busiest streets. This is just accepted: those with somewhere to go simply struggle past as best they can.

Driving

All in all, driving in cities is not to be recommended—unless your stay is going to be a long one, you are better off to avoid the stress by taking taxis. The satisfaction and comfort of driving a car is minimal and far outweighed by the eccentric driving habits of others, parking difficulties, the danger of theft, etc. Bolivian driving habits are abysmal: the horn is used instead of the brain. People park askew or stop abruptly in the middle of the road. The confined spaces and slopes of La Paz make speeding difficult, but in more level cities the streets can be dangerous. If you are exploring a remote area, however, having your own vehicle becomes a different proposition. Gasoline is far less expensive in Bolivia than in the USA or Europe.

Roadblocks mounted by *campesinos* and other groups are a worry for foreign embassies, but only occur at times of particular political stress. Check with your embassy before driving between the main cities—especially between La Paz, Cochabamba, and Santa Cruz.

WHERE TO STAY

The main cities offer accommodation for all budgets. Spartan but clean and quiet places are often available at very reasonable prices. The most expensive hotels are not always the best or the most relaxing: you may find yourself sharing a floor with a group of local businessmen out for a good time.

Posadas (inns) are the cheapest places, but not always the cleanest or most comfortable. A step up are *alojamientos*, still fairly basic but more acceptable. Then there is the upper end of the budget accommodation market—*residencias*, *casas de huéspedes* (guest houses), and *hostales*. But there is not much standardization or quality control, and if on a budget it's best to ask around among other travelers. Hotels also vary greatly in quality and price—information can be obtained through tourist offices.

Renting an Apartment

For those intending to stay for some time in Bolivia, its cities, like anywhere else, have their poorer and better-off districts. It is possible to rent an apartment through an agency or through word of mouth: get a lawyer to vet the lease. A Bolivian specialty is the *anticrético*, which entails lending a substantial sum against a property instead of paying rent. If the sum is not repaid, the lender keeps the house (again, not recommended without legal advice).

La Paz has its Zona Sur (Southern Zone), where both old and new wealth (diplomats, the military, executives, etc.) escape the chaos (and Indian migrants) of the increasingly shabby historic center and northern districts. Many foreigners live in Sopocachi, a picturesque but not exclusive area on the western slopes of the valley, within reach of the center. Some even live in El Alto, which is cheap and can be peaceful— advantages that must be weighed against the city's increasing crime rate and its distance from La Paz.

In Santa Cruz, which is laid out on a system of "rings" surrounding the old center, the wealthy areas like Country Club and Equipetrol are found in the outer fourth ring (*cuarto anillo*).

Many of Sucre's better-off residents still live
near the main square, as befits their seignorial
mentality: the central square has always been
demonstrably the seat of power in Latin American
cities, with government buildings sharing space
with the cathedral, police, and army buildings,
etc., and the richest inhabitants living nearby.
Sucre and Potosí are protected as UNESCO World
Heritage Sites. Cities without such safeguards,
such as La Paz and Oruro, are being ripped apart
to make way for the most bizarre approaches to
modernity—a condition longed for by many
Bolivians, who seem unaware of the cultural
implications of imitating the West. There is a
sense among the educated classes that Indian
newcomers to cities are erasing signs of a past
they find at best uncomfortable, at worst even a
persistent threat. In a rural context, one foreigner
asked why the Indians were destroying some of
the gracious *hacienda* houses that belonged to
those dispossessed after the 1952 Revolution. He
was told: the landowners might come back.

Domestics

Having an Indian woman in the house as an
empleada, or domestic, is seen as an automatic right
by the Bolivian upper classes, and is a vestige of the
quasi-feudal past. However, conditions are
changing: a minimum wage has been set (about US
$82 a month) though it is not always respected. Old
abuses are disappearing, such as the assumption

that male family members have sexual rights over the *empleada*.

Many Bolivian women wish to work as domestics. In more enlightened households the *empleada* may be regarded as a member of the family, her education allowed and even financed. But this is still rare, and most of these women long to work for foreigners, who are seen as better employers.

Use your common sense when choosing an *empleada*: not everyone is trustworthy, so ask around. It goes without saying that they must be treated with the utmost respect.

Class War

When the firebrand Indian leader Felipe Quispe was arrested in 1992 as a member of the short-lived Tupac Katari (EGTK) guerrilla movement, he famously replied to a journalist questioning his reasons for taking up arms: "So that my daughter will not become your maid."

A media uproar was unleashed in 2006 when the Morales government appointed Casimira Rodríguez, a woman who had once worked in domestic service, as Minister of Justice. Newspapers and TV argued that such a lowly figure was unsuitable for so lofty a position, but did not mention that Rodríguez had been an outstanding anthropology student supporting herself by her domestic work. She had also helped draw up a Domestic Workers' Law (establishing wages, hours, vacations, and other conditions) that was passed in 2003 in the face of considerable opposition.

HEALTH

The Bolivian state health service SUMI provides health services for women and children at minimal cost. This has recently been extended to senior citizens. Men are not protected in this way; they are seen as earning enough to pay for medical care.

Foreigners are advised to obtain health insurance coverage. Altitude sickness does not affect everyone, but it is best not to exert yourself on the first day at altitude. If arriving on a flight to La Paz, take it easy on the first day—even if you feel all right.

Yellow fever is a risk in the lowlands; the World Health Organization recommends vaccination. There are regular national vaccination campaigns, and people traveling to lowland areas are required to show proof that they have been vaccinated.

Chagas' disease (Trypanosomiasis humana) is transmitted by an insect known as the *vinchuca* that inhabits mud and cane dwellings below 9,843 ft (3,000 m). The incidence of Chagas' has been reduced by fumigation campaigns, but take advice if traveling to outlying tropical areas.

Malaria exists below 8,202 ft (2,500 m).

The incidence of rabies has been reduced by periodic vaccination campaigns during which people are invited to bring their pets (even street dogs are vaccinated: this is indicated by a green ribbon tied around their necks). Dogs in Bolivia are far less hostile than their counterparts in, for instance, Peru. Dogs roam city streets in sizeable packs, which can be intimidating at first, but they are not known to attack humans.

There has been no serious outbreak of cholera since the 1990s.

Drugs are often all too freely obtained in pharmacies without prescription. Some establishments are more scrupulous than others, of course; it is possible to obtain sound medical advice in pharmacies if you know where to go. Many poorer people and those of rural origin who are skeptical of Western medicine prefer to use "alternative" healing (recognized by the Ministry of Health). Again, check with local people beforehand, but Bolivia has a tradition of homeopathic and herbal treatment that goes back centuries. Such cures as coca-leaf tea for altitude sickness and stomach pains are universally approved. Anyone interested in such cures can go to the Mercado de Brujas (somewhat fancifully translated in guidebooks as the "Witchcraft Market") on Calle Santa Cruz in central La Paz, and consult the knowledgeable vendors. *Kallawaya* (traditional indigenous healers) are legendary, having

practiced since before Inca times with a compendious knowledge of herbs. They are based in the mountainous area north of La Paz, but are famous as itinerant healers.

SAFETY

Bolivia is not prone to natural disasters, though there are occasional floods. Earthquakes are rare apart from some areas around Cochabamba. Beware of extremes of heat and cold on the Altiplano: if you are backpacking or climbing, take light, protective wear as well as warm clothing. The highland sun is pitiless, so take a strong sunblock: it is not unusual to see gringos in La Paz with seriously sunburned noses and necks.

AIDS is not particularly widespread but, needless to say, unprotected sex is absolutely not recommended.

Unfortunately, crime is on the increase almost everywhere in the world. Bolivia is no exception, but you should enjoy your time and not feel threatened. Stay out of trouble by using common sense: above all, do not "rubberneck" distractedly in cities or tourist centers, especially if alone. Keep valuables out of sight and avoid poorer areas unless accompanied by a local. Avoid walking alone on deserted streets after dark.

You are advised to register at your embassy on arrival. Contact the Tourist Police (Plaza Tejada Sorzano, La Paz; tel. 222 5016) if the need arises.

"Secuestro Express" ("Express Kidnap")

Don't walk around with your credit cards on you. Once you've used your card to make a withdrawal, then leave it somewhere safe: it is becoming common for thieves to demand their victims' PIN numbers, even to kidnap the unwary for long enough to clear out their account.

MAIN TOURIST ATTRACTIONS

The following sights are unmissable for any visitor to Bolivia:

Lake **Titicaca** is only a few hours by bus from La Paz and is well worth a visit—even if only to contemplate the waters from one of the vantage points, such as the Cerro Calvario overlooking Copacabana.

Tiwanaku is also near La Paz; tours leave early and return the same day. One of Latin America's foremost archaeological sites, it has still to be fully excavated.

The **Uyuni** Salt Lake (Salar de Uyuni) is the largest in the world and is a spectacular experience that justifies the discomfort involved in travel to this remote area.

The beautifully restored **Jesuit Missions** in the Department of Santa Cruz are exquisite monuments to a more enlightened introduction of indigenous peoples to Christianity.

Another unique combination of outstanding historical importance and aesthetic value is **Potosí**, some seven hours by bus from La Paz, with some of the most fascinating American Baroque architecture in existence. This is the highly decorative style adopted after the conquest, when indigenous artisans applied their own motifs to the Christian churches, assimilating the new religious ambience. The number and splendor of religious buildings attest to the huge wealth of Potosí and the decadence this generated: those who got rich there built churches, both to give thanks to the Almighty and to cleanse their sins. The chronicles of Bartolomé Arzáns de Orsúa y Vela (see Further Reading: Padden 1975) are an invaluable testament to Potosí's decline.

La Paz is both beautiful and ugly, depending on your individual perspective and the part of town in question. The Museum of Ethnography (MUSEF) on Calle Ingavi is well worth a visit, having been imaginatively renovated in recent years. Some excellent paintings, both colonial and modern, can be seen in the National Art Museum on the Plaza Murillo (corner of Comercio and Socabaya).

Several museums on the pedestrian Calle Jaén (entrance is on one ticket) give an overview of various aspects of the country's history and culture. The area around Calle Jaén, with numerous museums and unspoiled streets, gives an idea of what the city would have been like had it been left intact.

Samaipata, some two hours from Santa Cruz on the Cochabamba road, is an intriguing pre-Columbian site made up of carvings on a huge rock atop a mountainside. The surrounding area is also worth exploring.

chapter eight

BUSINESS BRIEFING

Bolivia has a small population and a correspondingly small economy. It has no large companies (with capital of more than US $100 million). Otherwise, there are firms of all sizes, which for legal purposes fall into three categories: *unipersonal*, those with only one boss; *sociedad anónima*, headed by two or more people; and *responsabilidad limitada*, whose constitution guards against personal liability should the company fail.

It is advisable to check out the companies with which you plan to do business, either through the Web site of your country's embassy or the Bolivian Chambers of Commerce and Industry, or by finding out if they are registered with the

Federation of Private Impresarios (Fundempresa) or the Bolivian-American Chamber of Commerce. All but the smallest provincial companies have Web sites with relevant information.

Bolivia has made considerable efforts to improve its image abroad in recent years. This was one of the priorities of the Morales government, whose pragmatism seems to be bearing fruit. Diversification regarding trade partners responds to fluctuations in relations with the United States. George W. Bush suspended Bolivia's participation in the ATPDEA (Andean Trade Promotion and Drug Eradication Act) agreement, which relaxed import duties between the two countries. Bolivia is currently waiting to see what the Obama administration's attitude toward its southern neighbors will be. If unfavorable, Bolivia will be more reliant than ever on the links forged recently with Venezuela, China, Iran, and Cuba.

THE BUSINESS CULTURE

On the whole, Bolivians do not jealously guard information. Business is on a modest scale and even the larger entrepreneurs will make themselves available to the well-prepared visitor. Personal relationships are crucial in Bolivian business: individual influence goes a long way, and confidence in a company stems from mutual trust.

Business contacts are often made through trade fairs; the most important is Expocruz (Santa Cruz,

September). Another is Fexpo La Paz (late May–early June), run by a company specializing in business presentations. Smaller and more specialist trade fairs include Bolivia Telexpo for telecommunications, Gramma (agricultural produce), and FCB (Bolivian Scientific Foundation).

Modernity and Tradition
Bolivian companies are modernizing, but many smaller ones still have no e-mail or Web site. The lack of individual and home access to the Internet is reflected in the large number of Internet cafés.

Business practice is moving away from hierarchy and nepotism. But in the current economic climate, and given that educational levels are not the highest, parents who cannot afford to send their children to study abroad may offer them a place in the family firm. Whether this is at a level commensurate with their ability and experience depends on the company. A company's nature or internal politics, and openness to the idea of meritocracy, all depend largely upon those of its creators and leaders. The larger the company, the less personal its treatment.

Bolivia's major businesses are still either raw materials exporters, agricultural firms (soybeans, beef, and so on), or service industries; manufacturing is still limited.

Some companies diversify and adapt, such as the Monopolio paint company, which responded to its success by branching into cost-saving manufacture of the necessary plastic containers. Others, such as the jewelry firm Oro América, one of the biggest companies in La Paz, maintain their profits through continuing to rely on low labor costs.

"Something Extra"

The ancestral Andean practice of *yapa* has survived up to the present day. *Yapa*, a Quechua word, refers to the "little extra" that sweetens relations between market seller and client. Someone selling fruit juice in the market will offer an extra half-glass once you have drunk the first, thus ensuring your goodwill and further patronage. *Yapa*, however, can find its way into the business sphere too: a client may ask for another little task, tacked on to the original one. This is a fact of life, not corrupt practice; extra remuneration is neither asked for nor offered.

Formality

Foreigners are struck by the degree to which Bolivians address colleagues by their formal title or qualification: *Ingeniero* (engineer), *Licenciado* (holder of a B.A. or B.Sc.), *Doctor* (Ph.D.), and so on. The business environment is becoming more hierarchical; jobs are increasingly specialized as more people graduate in company administration, engineering, marketing, and other areas of business. Marketing sections are increasingly responsible for evaluating projects, while lobbying and public relations forge partnerships and associations with other companies. But when doing business in Bolivia, you should seek out the head of a company: the final decision always rests with the boss.

Dress Code

A suit and tie are required for business meetings in La Paz and western Bolivia generally, but in the Oriente this is more relaxed due to the heat. In Santa Cruz, for example, lighter clothes, casual but smart, are acceptable.

The dress code largely depends on the size and nature of the company concerned. At a large and important firm, dress will be formal. There are also codes depending on the profession concerned; the formality required by a law practice will naturally not apply to a rock promoter.

MEETINGS

Larger companies still operate with secretaries, offices, and the traditional business infrastructure. However, as with smaller companies, communication is increasingly done by e-mail: indeed, with the new virtual environment, many smaller businesses do not even have a physical address and are operated from a computer installed in a private home.

Of course, much of the groundwork should be done beforehand, through the Internet; once you have located a prospective company, you can write to them in English (most firms of medium size and upward have staff who can handle the language). Check the Web address: if it has a company name after the e-mail symbol then it is more reliable; if not, your message may well not arrive.

Bolivians are not known for their punctuality, but you will be expected to arrive on time for a business appointment.

When entering a meeting, shake hands with everyone. Men are expected to give women a kiss on the cheek—foreign women should not be surprised by this. Protocol demands that the senior partner in any encounter (executive, prospective investor) be the one to proffer his or her hand to be shaken, and this should be respected at least in formal situations (business, politics, the military, and so on).

However, precision and clarity of expression are often more important than observing strict protocol. Bolivians will make allowances for your unfamiliarity with their customs, but will not be pleased by an evasive manner, and busy executives will not want to listen to long-winded and meandering explanations.

Meetings in large, established firms are conducted with prearranged, written agendas and written minutes are kept. In smaller concerns, though, meetings will be far more informal: there will be no chairperson, the agenda will be improvised, and any record will be handwritten. In small companies meetings may be interrupted while the boss answers a phone call: in larger firms a secretary will usually deal with this.

PRESENTATIONS

PowerPoint is now the accepted medium for presentations in most professional spheres. However, a brief summary on paper is also expected: a condensed, one-page version that can be "eye-scanned" by a busy person who needs to make a quick decision.

Business presentations should be clear and concise, and last some fifteen to twenty minutes. A good sign that the customer is interested is if the session is significantly prolonged, but it should not be the person doing the presentation who extends the session. Bear in mind that much information is now available online; you can assume that a reasonably prepared workforce will be familiar with it.

The first presentation will be a general summary; subsequent data concerning international deals will be more detailed. Information regarding sources of funding might be best held back and perhaps only divulged to higher-ranking people. Larger firms prefer to mete out information at a meeting according to the rank of those present, and generally deny underlings access to material they may sell to other companies to supplement their earnings.

NEGOTIATIONS

It is best to adopt a harmonious negotiating style: Bolivians do not respond well to an aggressive approach. The same rules apply here as in market haggling: if buying, begin with a figure that is low, without being insulting; if selling, start high and progress from there. Bolivians can be evasive rather than frank, and don't always like saying no; they might respond to a derisory offer by asking for time to think it over, and never call back.

The need for courtesy cannot be too highly stressed, and misunderstandings due to cultural factors are possible between South American nationalities too. One Argentine visitor so disconcerted his Bolivian host with intemperate language and presumptuous behavior that the business relationship deteriorated beyond repair.

CONTRACTS

Business contracts follow the *Código Civil de Bolivia* (Bolivian Civil Code) based on the Roman legal system. Contracts must be translated from Spanish by an official translator accredited in Bolivia (embassies can advise) and validated by both the Chancellery and the visitor's embassy.

Previously established trust and guarantees are the best way of ensuring that a contract will be binding: check companies before you deal with them and have contracts vetted and signed by lawyers. A letter of credit can be signed, with the bank as intermediary. Arrangements can also be made for payment on delivery. Established Bolivian companies know one another and would be loath to risk damaging their image.

In the event of a dispute, conciliation is a far more common and sensible way of resolving matters than the stress and expense of going to court. The judicial process is fraught with delays and difficulties and is not entirely reliable: judges may be susceptible to corruption.

BUSINESS ENTERTAINMENT

Taking a prospective business partner out on the town for a meal and a drink is standard procedure, but should be done tactfully. Bolivians have no inhibitions about drinking and enjoying themselves. On the other hand, they are mindful of appearances, and would not want to come across as debauched to a puritanical gringo. They will take their cue from you. A good idea is to suggest moving a discussion from the office to the more relaxed atmosphere of a café, from where you can progress to dinner.

It is usual for the senior figure in the company to invite you home: accept the invitation, but do not show up until an hour or so after the agreed upon time. You should dress casually, and be prepared to talk about things other than business: this will be a strictly social occasion.

An important or inaccessible person can sometimes be found through their regular haunts. Someone who is unlikely to grant an office appointment can often be found in a more relaxed environment, asked for a business card, and subsequently e-mailed or contacted by phone.

You may be able to establish a relationship with a large and unreachable company by organizing a party ("*coctel*") for its top people in order to present your products. The person for whom the event is held will issue the host company with a guest list. Even if this does not result in a close link with the person targeted, those invited will offer a wealth of contacts. This approach may be adopted, fruitfully, with business attachés at embassies.

The closing of a deal will be marked by dinner at a stylish restaurant. If it is a particularly auspicious occasion, some companies will hire two or three rooms in a hotel and engage the services of a public relations company. The polished, professional demeanor and good looks of this company's employees are designed to enhance the reputation of the client firm: they employ people with honed communication skills, fluent in several languages, etc. While this is not strictly honest, as it is never made clear that the people in question are not from the client company, neither is it strictly lying.

CORRUPTION

Bribes often lubricate contact between private companies and officialdom. Within companies some corrupt practice may occur, for instance, in presenting artificially low sums on invoices to evade tax payment. There is no apparent reason for the visitor to become involved in any of this.

Gifts

It is, however, perfectly acceptable to give your Bolivian associate a gift when closing a deal. The era of gold pens is over. Today, high-quality drinks (whiskey, special-edition wines) are the most common gifts between businessmen, and the most warmly received.

BUREAUCRACY

Bolivian bureaucracy is not as fearsome as one might imagine. However, it is worthwhile getting a local expert, known as a *tramitador/tramitadora* (*trámite* means "red tape" in Spanish), to help with any red tape. Such people can normally be contacted through foreigners living in Bolivia who can recommend someone suitable. They have usually worked in government offices in some capacity, know people in the relevant places, and are able to get things done swiftly and painlessly. A good *tramitador/a* will not ask you to do anything illegal such as offering bribes.

WOMEN IN BUSINESS

The question of women in the workplace depends largely upon whom you talk to: it would appear that machismo is alive and well. For that reason visiting female executives can expect to be treated with respect, perhaps even with a degree of awe. However, signs that this is changing have appeared recently in various spheres. For example, there are Bolivian women at the head of concerns such as Yanbal cosmetics, the Andean Organic Food company Irupana, and the magazine *Cosas* (similar to the English-language *Hello*). Women are more likely to be employed in areas such as sales and human resources. If these are traditionally "feminine" products and interests, there are nevertheless signs of other barriers coming down: for instance, women heads of television companies, and the appointment of female colonels in the police force.

On the negative side, women are still affected by the overarching culture of machismo. In business, as elsewhere, they are automatically paid less than their male counterparts. No woman has been president of the Chamber of Commerce and women rarely rise above the rank of vice-minister.

COMMUNICATING

REGIONAL SPANISH AND *BOLIVIANISMOS*

Spanish is the most widely spoken of Bolivia's official languages (which also include Quechua, Aymara, and Guaraní). You should learn at least some Spanish before visiting the country; few Bolivians speak English or other European languages. Spanish is essential for basic everyday logistics, making friends other than expats, and gaining some understanding of the country.

Indigenous languages are mostly spoken in the countryside, Quechua mainly in the departments of Chuquisaca and Cochabamba. Aymara coexists with Quechua in those of La Paz and Oruro. Guaraní is spoken in the Chaco. Most people these days know their native language plus some Spanish, but this is not guaranteed in more remote areas. The lowland Oriente has many indigenous languages, some now spoken by tiny groups. Others, such as Bésiro in the Chiquitanía region, are being actively promoted and taught using modern methods.

All these languages have had a great influence on Bolivian Spanish, especially in the Andes where many Quechua and Aymara words find their way into daily speech. Aymara is strong in northern Bolivia, particularly in the cities of La Paz and El Alto (in Oruro both Aymara and Quechua are spoken). Syntax will sound particularly strange to outsiders, as well as the use of other distinctive grammatical constructions. Verb often comes after object: *frío hace* (cold it is) instead of *hace frío* (it's cold). Several words are taken directly from Aymara and used as slang: *macurca* (muscular pain); *ch'aki* (hangover); *k'encha* (bad luck); *chojcho* (tacky, kitsch).

Particular Bolivian terms reflect social reality and mock pretensions. *Chota-chola* is a woman of indigenous descent who abandons the native skirt (*pollera*) in favor of Western dress: hence she is perceived as having become neither one thing nor the other. A *birlocha* is a woman whose dyed hair betrays pretensions to "whiteness."

In Potosí and Sucre, even "white" people often speak Quechua: in these places it is still seen as a status symbol that allows communication with Indian "underlings." Spanish speakers are likely to pepper their speech with lexical borrowings, some showing local humor: *sonqo suwa* means a heartbreaker (literally, "heart-thief"); a *piki chaki* (literally, "flea legs") is a keen walker. In Cochabamba, endearments use the Quechua ending "*y*" (first person possessive):

wawitay (my baby), *mamitay* (my mama), and so on.

Santa Cruz speech omits consonants, especially the "*s*" in the middle or end of a word that tends to be aspirated, sounding more like an English "*h*" and making plurals resemble singular nouns. This is often transcribed as a "*j*" in Spanish: *puej*, for example, is the local slang form of *pues* (then, in that case). *Oí* is used instead of *oye* (listen).

Diminutives are very common throughout Latin America (far more than in Spain). Their most usual form is the suffix *–ito/-ita*, which conveys familiarity and fondness as well as small physical size. Thus *hermanito/a* is "little brother/sister." In the Santa Cruz area these suffixes are *–ingo/-inga*. *Pelado/pelada* and its diminutive *peladingo/peladinga* would translate as "little kid" in English.

Bolivian Spanish in the southwest shows evidence of the Guaraní language.

Some Mexican slang has made its way into everyday urban Bolivian speech, probably via the numerous television shows. *Chango* is used for a youth (even if its interpretation is different in Mexico). Argentine slang is even more common: *cana* (police, jail), *pucho* (cigarette), *trucho* (poor quality, a bad imitation) are but a few examples.

"Spanglish" is not as widely used as in other Latin American countries, but for recent inventions there are often no popularly used words in Spanish. *La laptop, el internet, el mouse* are among the most recent examples.

Other indigenous languages include Bésiro (Chiquitanía), Sirionó (Beni), and Ayoreo (Chaco): many of these tongues have very few speakers, and unfortunately are on the verge of extinction.

GREETINGS AND GOOD MANNERS

Bolivians are keen on formalities and greetings. *Buenos días* (good morning or good day), *buenas tardes* (good afternoon), and *buenas noches* (good evening or good night) are used when addressing anyone you do not know well. *Buenos días* applies up to midday; you may be corrected to *buenas tardes* if it is significantly later than noon. After nightfall, use *buenas noches*: this alone is used as a leave-taking. During the daytime you would say *adiós* or *hasta luego* (see you later).

If you ask hastily for directions in the street, you may be gently corrected and told to say *buenos días* first! It does not pay to be in a hurry, especially in La Paz. Sometimes the slightly informal abbreviation *buenas* is used.

POLITE FORMS OF ADDRESS

Failure to use these formalities can seem overfamiliar (*confianzudo*).

The use of *señor/señora/señorita* is the most common form of address, even among younger people who don't know each other. *Caballero* (equivalent to "gentleman") is still more polite, and may be used in shops and elsewhere. For people who are worthy of particular respect, *don* or *doña* is used with the first name. Some greetings between older people are charmingly florid but can seem rather quaint, such as *mucho gusto en saludarlo* (akin to "delighted to see you"). More familiar and intimate greetings, used between younger people and friends, are "*¿cómo es?*" or "*¿qué tal?*" (roughly equivalent to "how's it going?" or "how are you doing?").

Spanish, like other Romance languages, has formal and informal second-person pronouns. Older people or those in positions of authority would automatically be addressed using the formal *usted* and its corresponding verb conjugations. However, *tú* would be automatically used between younger people or among those (bohemian, artistic) for whom informality is taken for granted. Another informal pronoun is *vos*, rarely used with a verb; if learning Spanish you should recognize it but not worry about conjugations. Second-person plural is always *ustedes*; never the Iberian Spanish *vosotros*.

Among close friends *hermano/hermana* (brother/sister) is commonly used. Also popular in Bolivia is *che* (pal, mate), the form of address immortalized in Ernesto "Che" Guevara, who was given this nickname because *che* is inextricably associated with his native Argentina, though it originally comes from Valencia (Spain). It is an endearment that has been used for centuries in Bolivia, as well as Argentina and Uruguay.

Maestro is often used for people such as taxi drivers, plumbers, and so on who have the distinction of mastering a manual trade and, although not having an academic qualification, have overcome the barriers of class.

In markets it is common for sellers to make an effort to strike up a relationship with customers, to ensure they return on a regular basis. The form of address employed once this kind of rapport is established is *casero/casera* (used for a regular customer).

The title "*Doctor*" is applied, erroneously, to people who have graduated with a first degree in medicine, dentistry, or veterinary studies. It is also wrongly applied to those minimally qualified in law, but doubtless reflects the awe in which lawyers, judges, and the like are held. Similar status-inflation was practiced by Goni and his vice president, Víctor Hugo Cárdenas, who styled themselves "*licenciado*" until forbidden to do so by the university (UMSA) in La Paz, from which they had failed to graduate.

Domestics or other people engaged in some kind of service will often use *joven* to address the youngest man of the family. The word literally means "young man," but in this case implies the status of heir. A man might be spoken to by door attendants using the slightly ironic but nonetheless respectful *jefe* (chief).

Manners

The Bolivian level of politeness, especially in the Andes, may appear quaint in other areas of Latin America. Once during a short stay in the Dominican Republic after being in Bolivia, my elaborate La Paz-style blandishments were met with stony, puzzled gazes and pithy replies of ¡hola!

Bolivians are not particularly given to swearing, and are sometimes shocked by the level of profanity used by Argentines, Spaniards, and Mexicans. Bolivians who live for some time in these countries, and have children there, are often taken aback by their offspring's colorful outbursts. For example, the Argentine term of endearment to parents, *viejo/vieja* (old man/woman), is something they wouldn't dream of using.

Foreign names can be difficult for Bolivians not used to Anglo-Saxon and other spellings, or pronunciation. Some foreigners find it helps to adapt their name to something a bit more Spanish-sounding. You may find your name wrongly spelled: don't be offended by this, but be sure to correct it, particularly on official documents.

BODY LANGUAGE

Physical closeness is inevitable in Bolivian cities, given the crowded streets and particularly the buses, intended for people somewhat smaller than the average gringo. People are not particularly tactile, especially in the Andes.

The Latin trait of speaking with the hands is more common in the Italian-influenced Plate River area than in the rest of Bolivia: however, some gestures are widespread. Empty-handedness is indicated by swiveling one hand at the wrist, with the fingers spread apart to show they hold nothing. A similar gesture, but with fingers together and pointing downward, says "I am/we are leaving." Other hand movements seem familiar to Westerners but with variations: the beckoning gesture is made with the palm facing downward. Like most Latin Americans, Bolivians count using the little finger first, rather than the thumb. Traders often use the V-sign simply to indicate the number two, which may be unsettling for visitors accustomed to a ruder meaning.

THE MEDIA
The Press
The MAS government has not founded a mouthpiece for its avowed revolutionary aims. This means that the Bolivian daily press is mainly antigovernment. Paradoxically, given the political climate, many left-wing journalists have taken

up political positions, diplomatic posts, etc., complaining of the deterioration in professional standards as well as changes in political orientation as the press becomes more conservative.

The main daily newspapers in La Paz are *La Prensa* and *La Razón*: both are right wing and privately owned. You may get a wider range of opinion from simply talking to people. *Época* is a free pro-government paper and *Pulso* is right of center but thoroughgoing. Other newspapers, all conservative, are *El Diario* (La Paz), *Los Tiempos*, *Opinión* (Cochabamba), *El Deber* (Santa Cruz), *El Correo del Sur* (Sucre), and *El Nuevo Día* (Santa Cruz).

Television

There is a range, albeit limited, of political opinion. Among the national stations, Canal 7 (Channel 7), the only government mouthpiece, and ATV, the fiercest of many opposition stations, represent opposite ends of the political spectrum. Bolivian television is not of a very high standard and produces little in the way of original programming. Two welcome exceptions are *Sin Letra Chica* (*With No Small Letters*), daily political analysis on the P.A.T. channel by the controversial journalist Carlos Valverde, who offers more than simply the party line from his native Santa Cruz, strives to remain neutral, and is always thought provoking. Another enormously popular character is the *chola* presenter La Justa, whose daily cookery show on Canal 7 strays into some often interesting commentary, stimulated by viewers' phone-ins, about the current situation in the country.

Radio

This medium, which is often less subservient to big financial interests, is a means of reaching people in remote rural areas with no electricity supply. ACLO (Acción Loyola, Sucre) is one of several Jesuit-run stations that give the *campesinos* a voice. FIDES is a national chain of stations run by the Jesuits (including Radio Laser, one of the few stations broadcasting classical music). Radio Erbol is the other main national station. Radio Pachamama, which broadcasts from El Alto, has news and interviews from a popular perspective. Radio París has a service in French.

Radio stations were not common until the National Revolution in 1952. As in Revolutionary Cuba, rural audiences took on a new importance: numerous radio stations grew up to inform and influence the previously ignored *campesinos* as well as little-heeded miners.

Radio has also taken on the role of safeguarding indigenous culture from Western and urban influences. Some stations broadcast entirely in Aymara or Quechua, allowing Indian communities to hear their own languages in a broader context. An example of this is the Jesuit station ACLO, whose broadcasts aim to improve awareness in various fields: good agricultural procedures, health care, and political consciousness as well as providing news, music (including an annual provincial music festival), and other topics aimed at preserving cultural self-esteem.

Radio has played an important political role, largely because of the ease with which transistors can be bought and carried. Radio stations were important disseminators of information during the miners' strikes. The vicious dictatorship of Luis García Meza in the early 1980s targeted radio stations for repression, obliging them to broadcast "official" news reports.

MAIL

The Correo Central, or main post office, is where you will normally pick up mail *poste restante* (general delivery). It may help to ask correspondents to underline your surname, particularly if it is one that might be confused with a first name (Richards, for example!).

The Bolivian state postal service is not as efficient as it once was: parcels might take a month to arrive from Europe. Letters usually take ten days from Europe or the United States. However, most people's experience of the best-known private mailing services is that they are far more expensive but are no better as regards speed or reliability. If you need to send something with absolute confidence, it might be better to find someone traveling and ask them to act as courier.

TELEPHONES

Call centers are plentiful and easy to use. You should ask the prices before you phone as they vary considerably. Some Web-based telephone centers are extremely cheap. The state company Entel, once capitalized under Goni, has been renationalized; Viva is now the private option.

Cell phones are very popular and it is not unusual to see indigenous people using them. Your own phone may well be adaptable for local use. It is not difficult to get a landline installed, though cell phones are quicker. If you do not have your own phone you can easily find one on the street, either land (*fijo*) or cell (*celular*), at little cost. If phoning long distance, it is worth looking for places that offer calls through the Internet.

INTERNET

Many homes do not have Internet—a fact reflected in the popularity of cybercafés (*un internet* in Spanglish), a cheap and good service, at least in cities, and the best way of keeping in touch with people and events back home. For Bolivians, it encourages literacy as well as being a window to the outside world.

CONCLUSION

Bolivia is going through profound and rapid change, after a long period of relative stagnation in which repression and social exclusion had created a society comparable to apartheid-era South Africa. This dynamic situation is a both a challenge and a source of excitement for the visitor; another is Bolivia's kaleidoscopic cultural diversity, which is at last being recognized and assimilated into national life.

Bolivia is not the easiest place to study or get to know, and neither are its people the most straightforward. The outsider, however curious or well-intentioned, can find them at times frustrating, incomprehensible, even exasperating. But there is certainly a welcome for everybody who is prepared to take the time and trouble to understand, rather than judge them according to Western precepts. The independent-minded visitor will be rewarded by getting to know a people whose sense of self-worth has survived decades of oppression. Whether your trip is work-related or a journey of discovery, it is impossible not to be affected by this extraordinary country.

Further Reading

Bakewell, Peter. *Miners of the Red Mountain: Indian Labor in Potosí, 1545–1650.* Albuquerque: University of New Mexico Press, 1984.

Chungara, Domitila, and Moema Viezzer. *Let Me Speak! Testimony of Domitila, a Woman of the Bolivian Mines.* New York: Monthly Review, 2006.

Cole, Jeffrey A. *The Potosí Mita, 1573–1700: Compulsory Indian Labor in the Andes.* Stanford, Calif.: Stanford University Press, 1985.

Dunkerley, James. *Rebellion in the Veins: Political Struggle in Bolivia, 1952–1982.* London: Verso, 1984.

Gott, Richard. *Land Without Evil: Utopian Journeys Across the South American Watershed.* London: Verso, 1993.

Harris, Olivia. "The Eternal Return of Conversion: Popular Christianity in Highland Bolivia." In *The Anthropology of Christianity*, edited by Fenella Cannel. Durham, NC: Duke University Press, 2006.

Klein, Herbert S. *Bolivia: the Evolution of a Multi-Ethnic Society.* Oxford/New York: Oxford University Press, 1992.

Padden, R. C. (ed). *Tales of Potosí.* Providence, RI: Brown University Press, 1975.

Reyes, Sandra, John Dival, and Gastón Fernández (eds). *Oblivion and Stone: A Selection of Contemporary Bolivian Poetry and Fiction.* Ozark: University of Arkansas, 1998.

Richards, Keith John (compiler). *Narrative from Tropical Bolivia/Narrativa del trópico boliviano.* Santa Cruz, Bolivia: La Hoguera, 2004.

Young, Rusty. *Marching Powder.* London: Macmillan, 2004.

Useful Web Sites

Press and Media
www.periodicopukara.com/
www.pulsobolivia.com/
www.laprensa.com.bo/
www.lostiempos.com/
www.eldeber.com.bo/
correodelsur.com/2008/0920/cj

Films and Documentaries
Cocalero. Alejandro Landes, Argentina/Bolivia, 2006
The Devil's Miner. Kief Davidson and Richard Ladkani, USA/Germany, 2006.
First Run/Icarus Films
www.thedevilsminer.com
Our Brand is Crisis. Rachel Boynton, USA, 2005
www.ourbrandiscrisis.net/
Radio Pachamama
www.radiopachamama.com/

Doing Business in Bolivia (US Embassy)
http://spanish.cochabamba.usvpp.gov/uploads/images/cpKdBDX7yebq58BE
XGqsog/CCommGuide2007.pdf

Index

Acknowledgments

I would like to thank the following people for their invaluable help in researching this book: Pilar Andreu, Beatiz Lizarazu, Ruth Mérida, Néstor Taboada Terán, and Jansen Vow.